THE PRAISE OF FOLLY

The spirit of Erasmus wanders through what was Rotterdam

THE PRAISE OF FOLLY

BY **Desiderius Erasmus**

OF ROTTERDAM

WITH A SHORT LIFE OF THE AUTHOR BY

Hendrik Willem van Loon

OF ROTTERDAM

WHO ALSO ILLUSTRATED THE BOOK

PUBLISHED FOR THE CLASSICS CLUB

BY WALTER J. BLACK OF NEW YORK

Dedication
to Elmer Davis

Dear Elmer:

You undoubtedly remember that hideous day when you and I, with horror in our hearts, sat before a map of the town of Rotterdam and watched the gradual and systematic destruction of that ancient city by Adolf Hitler's henchmen, intent upon "teaching the rest of the world a lesson it would not forget," as indeed it won't, for quite a good many centuries to come. And you will recollect that at one moment I suddenly lapsed into my native vernacular and you, though ignorant of that tongue, inquired what it might have been that I said and that even to the ignorant ear sounded like the most unstinted malediction you had ever heard.

DESIDERIUS ERASMUS

I told you that a few minutes before the conflagration must have reached the statue of Erasmus and that by this time it must have crossed the market place and must have wiped out the house in which that great and good man had seen the light of day. Then you looked at me with some surprise and said, "My dear Hendrik, you hardly could have expected Adolf to be very particular about him, now could you?" And I had to confess that you were right. For there is no room on this earth for the spirit of Desiderius Erasmus and for Adolf Hitler, and so the Dutchman had to go. At least, for a little while and until the Führer shall have become a moth-eaten dummy in some obscure Bavarian wax-works.

Now if we ever hope to win this war (which we have got to do, as life in a world dominated by the philosophy of Nazism would be worse than death), we must first of all stake out a very different social order from the one to which we are bidding farewell just now and which, no matter from what angle we look at it, is simply not good enough for decent human beings wishing to live simple, decent lives. But what kind of world should succeed it? That is what we should try and find out right now, and for this purpose we have revived a very old little pamphlet, a

VIII

small booklet which is only eighteen years younger than Columbus' four-page report upon his discovery of a new continent.

We brought it back to life because we thought that it would come in very handy at the next peace conference, for we feel (as so many other people do) that if a copy of *The Praise of Folly* had lain at the side of all the delegates at the conference of Versailles, this might indeed be a very different world from what it is today—that is, if they had felt inclined to read the little *opusculum* and to familiarize themselves with the ideas that spooked around in the brain of that witty old Dutchman with the long nose and the twinkling eyes who worked eighteen hours a day for almost sixty years while endlessly complaining that he never felt quite well.

Arises the question—what were those ideas which inspired him to undertake his Herculean task? I think that I can sum them all up in one single sentence. He wanted mankind to be set free from fear and disaster by being set free from its own ignorance; he hoped for a world in which intelligence, common sense, good manners, tolerance, and forbearance should dominate the scene instead of violence, ignorance, prejudice and greed. We now realize that he made a fatal mistake which prevented him

from being victorious. Like most of his contemporaries he
started from the wrong end. He began with the top of the
pyramid of enlightenment, whereas he should have begun
with the bottom. Of course, that plan too may not work.
But we have never yet tried it very seriously. Why not
begin now? It may take a few thousand years, but better
waste a little time than be doomed forever to live in a
potential Paradise converted into a dog-kennel.

When I had finished my humble share as commentator
and illustrator to this modest opus, I suddenly had an idea.
I have come to know my beloved Erasmus pretty well during the last thirty-five years. And I thought, suppose that
somewhere in a quiet corner of Heaven the old gentleman
sits and whiles away the tedious hours of his enforced
idleness by occasionally tuning in on the latest news that
arrives from his former place of abode, what would he say
of it all?

Most of his comment, I am afraid, would be lost to
you because he shared my habit of falling into his native
tongue whenever he was greatly pleased or deeply dis-
tracted. But he would add that now and then, when there
was not too much static (Berlin trying to jam the H.B.S.),
he had heard some comment which seemed to make so

X

much sense that he would have dearly liked to meet the person who belonged to the voice that spoke into the mike.

You, my dear Elmer, happen to be that voice and that man, and for that reason I beg to place your name on the dedicatory page of this book with all the friendship and affection of

Yours as ever,

Henricus Rotterodamus.

Contents

Illustrations
for
DESIDERIUS ERASMUS

XV

DESIDERIUS ERASMUS

XVI

Illustrations
for
THE PRAISE OF FOLLY

XVII

XVIII

XIX

DESIDERIUS ERASMUS

DESIDERIUS ERASMUS

Concerning the background and personality of the famous scholar and author of The Praise of Folly, *Dr. Desiderius Erasmus of Rotterdam*

GOOD READER, I envy you in case this is the first time this charming booklet has been brought to your attention.

Now that I have passed three score, I am beginning to discover that much that had been told me in Reproach of Old Age was not so. It is true that for quite a long time the mirror has revealed a steady diminution of the hirsute pride of my younger days. The dentist's bills too increase rapidly but they are what one might call "final bills," for the upkeep of my new and artificial ivories is insignificant compared to the maintenance of the genuine article in the

3

days when I still was in full possession of all my molars and bicuspids.

I have also become aware of a gradual decline in the violence of those devastating emotions which caused an otherwise sensible citizen to waste so much time upon the pursuit of certain ideals of female pulchritude which were apparently unattainable on this faulty planet of ours. But these disturbing passions are now being replaced by certain far more satisfying sentiments of true comradeship and sincere affection which are the reward of that rather bizarre quest for the One Perfect Individual.

There also came a very noticeable indifference about such silly trivialities as catching trains, attending opening nights of new plays, or being among those present at what were supposed to be "important social gatherings." And that comfortable and familiar chair by the fire, watching the antics of Noodle, the dachshund, and Patent Leather, the black kitten, proved to be infinitely more comfortable than seat A-2, provided for his honored guest by Maestro Edward Johnson of the Metropolitan Opera Company or the manager of the latest popular play. Besides, I had already heard all of Johnson's little operas until I had come to know them by heart, and as for an evening at the playhouse, it meant putting on a rather uncomfortable shirt and eating a hasty meal at an unreasonable hour and in the end, would the mummers show me anything I had not seen long before or would ever care to see again?

No, I am here to state, and as emphatically as I can, that all the usual bugaboos about the Horrors of Advancing Years have proved to be mere chimerae and that I do not want to go back by one single year along the road which has carried me to my present state of incipient old age.

But I have one sincere complaint against the Great Arranger of our Fate in regard to the state of senectitude. I have spent more than half a century reading books. I have read them in half a dozen languages and in translations of those originally published in Finnish, Hungarian, Chinese or in Gertrude Stein's quaint vernacular, and their contents have been duly noted if not always overmuch enjoyed.

And now I find myself face to face with the terrible problem of "What in Heaven's name can I read that I have not already read a dozen times before?" The modern output is like a mighty river. At certain spots it is a veritable Rio de la Plata, almost fifty miles wide but so shallow that even crossing it in a rowboat throws up such quantities of mud that it begins to resemble the mighty Missouri in spring.

I therefore got in the habit of, whenever possible, returning to the much more attractive little creeks of the hinterland of my youth; but these I have visited so often that I have gradually come to know them by heart and I will never again experience the inexpressible joy of coming upon some new discovery, of passing with bated breath by some unexpected cliff at the other side of which there stretched a landscape as refreshing and as unexpected as the valleys and mountain peaks of the delectable land of Erewhon.

And that, good reader, is the true curse of advancing age. There are no fresh authors to whom one can turn for solace and delectation. There are no new books to be read, and without new books and unknown authors, life indeed has lost a great deal of its charm.

I therefore envy the reader who will now for the first time make the acquaintance of Desiderius Erasmus and of that piece of highly explosive literary dynamite known the last four centuries and a half as *The Praise of Folly*.

A PERSONAL INQUIRY among my more intimate friends and neighbors (and Old Greenwich rightfully prides itself upon its high percentage of college graduates) revealed Erasmus as "that old fellow with the long nose," as a Saint, as a "friend of Luther" or as "somebody who was all for tolerance but who would not fight for it." Less erudite neighbors confused him with the inventor respectively of the thermometer and the telescope. A chance acquaintance on the 5:08 mistook this most clear-headed of all Renaissance thinkers for the muddle-headed Nostradamus, the French-Jewish physician who is supposed to have predicted the rise and fall of Herr Adolf Hitler four centuries before that unfortunate Slavic-Teutonic half-breed had seen the light of day. And one B.A. of recent vintage thought that Erasmus was the man who had written a book about an illegitimate child who had spent his days making little round Dutch cheeses in the ancient city of Ter Gouw.

It may therefore serve a useful purpose if I present you with a few of the more important facts concerning the life of my famous fellow townsman. I think that I have come to know him about as well as any of the other writers who have devoted their time and energy to reconstructing this strange figure who did more than any other word-juggler to upset the Church of the early half of the sixteenth century, yet was held in such profound esteem by the occupant of the Holy See that, had he so desired, he could have died a cardinal with an official funeral at the expense of the Vatican.

It will be a delicate subject, for Erasmus was a complicated creature, composed of more contradictions than one would deem it possible to find in a single individual. But I am sure that (our personal relationship being what it is) he won't take it amiss if I endeavor to represent him as he really was. His bones now rest in the good city of Basel. His statue in our native city was destroyed by the Barbarians when two years ago they burned down our native habitat. Nothing therefore remains but his memory.

It so happens that I revere that memory. For whenever I am asked in what kind of a world I would like best of all to live, my answer is all ready: "Turn me loose in a universe re-created after the Erasmian principles of tolerance, intelligence, wit, and charm of manner and I shall ask for no better."

SHOULD YOU, most welcome reader, after these few exhortatory remarks, still feel inclined to open the pages of *The Praise of Folly,* which follow immediately afterwards, I think that I can foretell with a great degree of certainty exactly what your first reactions will be. In spite of the somewhat antiquated language of this little book, which we have retained on purpose, that you may understand the old gentleman all the better, you will be struck by the surprisingly "modern approach" of one who has been in his grave for more than four centuries. And in the second place, you will throw your arms up in great and serious astonishment and you will exclaim, "But this cannot be true!" No one in his senses would have dared to write this sort of thing at a moment when the Inquisitor was in his heyday and when no one was safe from the spiritual Gestapo of the sixteenth century. He must have realized that the publication of such a wholesale attack upon the existing order of things would have meant his immediate disappearance in a deep dark dungeon from which he would not have emerged until the executioner knocked at his door to conduct him roughly to the scaffold. Even today such a furious blast against established authority would hardly be tolerated. But we no longer burn those with whom we disagree; we merely leave them to the mercies of a very cheerless economic fate.

Let me at once put your mind at rest upon that particular point. Even His Holiness the Pope, who came in for a fine lambasting, experienced unalloyed delight while reading those ominous pages. The Emperor Charles, although he was not exactly a lover of what were called *belles lettres,* found nothing in this tract to call for his man of the law and to order an investigation with the usual disastrous results for the over-bold author. Indeed, speaking entirely from memory, I seem to remember that there were only two institutions of the higher learning which made some kind of effort to suppress this contribution to the hilarity of nations. One was the University of Louvain, which not only Erasmus but all the more liberal theologians of that age held in small esteem as a hotbed of reactionary tendencies. The other was the Sorbonne whose record as a stronghold of spiritual and political conservatism was so well established that its disapproval attracted very little attention—all the more so as the King was known to be entirely on the side of the author.

Here we come face to face with the interesting question: How could this possibly happen in a world which was still entirely dominated by the Church—which was still essentially dominated by the medieval conception of life—which accepted its religious experiences as an integral part of its daily existence and not as something about which one got interested only on Sunday at eleven o'clock in the morning? I think that the answer is implied in the question. People had not yet become self-conscious about their religious sentiments. They could therefore indulge in a discussion of the shortcomings of their Church with the same aloof interest with which we of today are able to discuss the problems of modern education or public hygiene. All of us know that much is wrong with our pedagogical system and that the care bestowed upon the sick and the mentally deficient could be infinitely improved. And we realize that a thoroughgoing discussion is absolutely necessary if we ever wish to bring about reform.

Also, please keep in mind that *The Praise of Folly* was written several years before Luther openly defied the Church and that no one until then had ever dreamed of even the most remote possibility of the Western Church being divided into two hostile factions. Criticism therefore, even criticism as bitter and poignant as that which you will find in Erasmus' pamphlet, was still essentially a domestic affair. The fight between the different parties which clamored for reform was really a family quarrel.

Family quarrels, as all of us realize only too well, are apt to be very bitter. But being family quarrels, everybody also knows that no matter what is said or done in the heat of argument, the family as such will continue to stick together as a unit. The last thing Erasmus had in mind when he so brilliantly and bitterly exposed the dreadful shortcomings of the Church of his day, and of a society that was still completely dominated by that most powerful organization, was to provoke an open breach between those who wanted to maintain the ancient *status quo* and those who had warned that, unless some drastic changes were brought about quickly, there soon would be no chance of a satisfactory compromise.

In the opinion of most modern critics it was *The Praise of Folly* which did more than almost any other printed volume to cause that spiritual rebellion which Protestants now know as the Reformation and which from the Catholic point of view has always remained a schism rather than a reform. But Erasmus, who composed his popular treatise while still smarting under the things he himself had witnessed in the Holy City and everywhere else in Italy, could no more guess what far-reaching developments the immediate future held in store than Jean-Jacques Rousseau could have anticipated the cataclysmic results of his sentimental meditations upon the "Perfect Man of the Future." Erasmus merely wrote of certain things which at that moment needed to be said in public. And it is from this angle that you must read his book if you really want to understand and appreciate it.

"This world as it is being lived just now has become a complete absurdity," was all Erasmus intended to convey.

"Allow me, therefore, my friends, to call upon the Goddess of Folly to explain to you how our religious, political, and social fabric has now assumed proportions of such grotesque stupidity and imbecility that only a complete fool can any longer hope to be happy while living under this kind of dispensation."

As the vast majority of those of his contemporaries who could think for themselves shared his views, his modest literary effort was bound to become an instant and widespread success. There were undoubtedly a few old stick-in-the-muds and incorrigible reactionaries who angrily shook their heads and warned against that delightful bit of prose which pretended to be no more than harmless clowning but which contained greater explosive potentialities than a whole cellarful of villainous saltpeter. These, however, were immediately overruled by the others, who said, "Oh, why not let us have a nice laugh at ourselves? We should not always take everything too seriously and a bit of good clean fun has never done anyone any harm."

The latter opinion usually prevailed. *The Praise of Folly* was not suppressed. It went through endless editions, and was translated into almost every civilized tongue. It has remained practically the only small social pamphlet which has come down to us from the days of the Renaissance, having survived in spite of a style which even the most ardent admirers of Erasmus must consider to be slightly out of date.

That, in itself, is an achievement which deserves more than passing praise, especially when we remember that this was an age when everybody was having his little say upon the evils of his time. But of all those literary products of the early quarter of the sixteenth century *The Praise of Folly* and Thomas More's *Utopia* are the ones best known today. And Erasmus' booklet far surpasses More's work in current popularity, for the simple reason that it made no claim to be anything more than it was. Far from being an appeal to revolution, it merely called attention to certain intolerable conditions which demanded the attention of competent authorities.

But while everybody was more than willing to laugh at the follies Erasmus pictured, very few people felt inclined to act. Erasmus had done the best he could do. Toward the end of his long life, and after the break he had feared had actually occurred, he became painfully conscious of his failure to achieve that which he had set out to accomplish. What else could he have expected? What other fate has ever overtaken the true pioneers of the human spirit?

14

I HAVE A FRIEND who is a composer. Living as he does in the twentieth century, he is obliged to pay the landlord, the butcher and the fur coat maker by writing musical fodder for the public that listens to radio commercials. His output is enormous but he always looks as fresh as the proverbial daisy. One evening when, as usual, we had met at the modern equivalent of Plato's ancient academy, the drugstore on the ground floor of N.B.C. where all the aerial sages meet for hamburgers, coffee, and ham-on-rye, I commented upon the industry he had displayed during the previous six months, and I said, "You must be exhausted! All this endless music must have taken a lot out of you."

"Lord help me, no!" he answered in great glee. "I don't feel tired at all. But I confess that it has taken an awful lot out of Mendelssohn and Mozart and Tschaikowsky."

I am reminded of this little anecdote because nowadays, whenever I am presented with still another of those biographies which have been so popular these last ten years, I am apt to feel that it must have taken an awful lot out of the Britannica, the Grande Larousse and the even bigger Brockhaus.

I should not, I presume, give away the secrets of our trade (or is ours a profession?) but I will state as emphatically as I can that none of our magnificent handbooks of Ready Reference have suffered at all on account of this short introduction to the Life and Times of Desiderius of Rotterdam. In case you are addicted to a diet of dates, you had better try your luck with "Information Please" and get a free copy of the British Encyclopedia. For I shall merely indulge in a "background picture." Having known the old gentleman, and rather intimately, for more than fifty years, I feel that I can talk about him as if he had been my own grandfather, or my uncle, who, when I last heard of him, was still alive, although Herr Hitler may have let him starve or freeze to death in the meantime.

When did I first make his acquaintance? A little over half a century ago, and in quite a natural manner. Shortly after my fifth birthday it was decided that I should be made to take the first steps along the road that was to lead me eventually towards the delectable garden of the Muses. And so, every morning at twenty minutes before nine I was entrusted to the care of old Hein, our man of all work, that I might be guided safely and decorously to that establishment of Higher Learning where I was to be given instruction in the art of weaving paper mats and how to place alphabet blocks in their right sequence. And every morning at ten minutes before nine, Hein and I passed

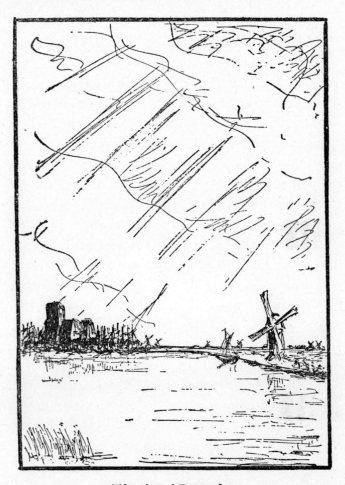

The city of Rotterdam

underneath the shadow of the ancient and honorable church of St. Lawrence and caught sight of the noble statue which the grateful people of Rotterdam had erected in memory of their most distinguished citizen.

There he stood, Desiderius Erasmus Rotterdamus, facing the humble house in which he had seen the light of day, deeply engrossed in turning over the leaf of the heavy metal book which he carried in his left hand. I had not the slightest idea who Des. Erasmus Rot. ob.A.D. MDXXXVI might have been, nor why he should have deserved to be commemorated in this imposing manner. No use asking questions, for old Hein, like most of the people of his social antecedents who inhabited the city of my birth, had not the slightest idea who he had been. They knew that Jan Rasmus, as he was popularly called, had been dead a great many years. But what exactly he had done to deserve such a superior honor (for the people of Rotterdam were not much given to hero-worship connected with the expenditure of public funds) was not quite clear to them. They vaguely associated him with one of the lesser heroes of the great war of independence against Spain, but those eighty years of uninterrupted fighting had produced such a large crop of outstanding men and women that one of them (like this iron figure in the long, flowing robe) could quite easily have gone aſtray in their memories. And so it was vaguely accepted that he had been some kind of dominie, probably one of the leaders of the Reformation. That would account for the big book in his hand, which was unmiſtakably a Bible. It was this book which fascinated me moſt of all. For when Jan Rasmus heard the clock ſtrike the hour, he was said to turn a leaf. Every morning, therefore, I begged old Hein to let me wait in front of my silent friend until the clock of old St. Lawrence should announce the hour of nine and I could bear witness to the eagerly expeꞓted leaf-turning. School, however, was school in the Holland of my youth, and since at nine o'clock I was supposed to be in the classroom, I was never able to watch this miracle in which I believed as firmly as in the exiſtence of St. Nicholas.

It was not until a great many years later that I discovered the truth. Erasmus did indeed turn a leaf of his book when-ever he heard the clock ſtrike, but being made of iron and not of ordinary human flesh and blood, he was unable to hear anything at all.

And so Erasmus had his firſt little joke on me when I was five and when he had been in his grave for more than three centuries and a half, and that was only the beginning.

At school we did not learn very much about him. This

was only natural. Children love heroes and Erasmus was not exactly a hero. What he might have done if ever he had been faced with the problem of dying for his beliefs, we do not know. Perhaps he would have displayed as much courage as did his friends Thomas More and John Fisher, and would have gone to the scaffold with equal fortitude in the knowledge that by his act he was setting an example of moral righteousness. But he was primarily an artist and therefore knew that in nature the intermediary colors predominate and an absolute white and an absolute black are rarely found.

He recognized that this lack of a definite differentiation also prevailed within the realm of the spirit and never could quite make up his mind where absolute right bade farewell to absolute wrong. In consequence whereof he became the ideal follower of the middle-of-the-road, and such people have never achieved the same popularity as those who, like Luther or Calvin, proclaimed exactly where they stood and thereupon defied all the devils in Hell to come and make them move an inch from the position they had chosen for themselves.

In a country like ours where men, women, children, and all other domestic and wild animals were fully conscious of their rights and spent most of their lives defending them against real and imaginary enemies, the pliable and malleable mentality of Erasmus could not possibly be appreciated at its true value.

When I was young, the debate started three centuries before by the learned Doctors of Theology, Martinus Luther and Ioannes Calvin, had by no means abated but was continuing with all its ancient fury and violence. The more enlightened classes of society were almost to a man (and a woman) determined followers of the tolerant enlightenment of the eighteenth century. But the "common people," who continued to dwell in a hermetically sealed little world of their own, still engaged in heavy and protracted debates upon such rather abstruse subjects as infant damnation and predestination.

But Erasmus had consistently refused to take sides in quarrels of this sort because he felt they belonged to the realm of the spirit and could therefore never be settled by the application of human reason. As a result, he was held in rather low esteem by the majority of my neighbors, and in the primary schools he was rarely mentioned except in his capacity of a distinguished man of letters. But since "letters" as such rarely interest children of ten, the greatest classical scholar of the out-going Middle Ages and the early part of the Renaissance completely failed to fire our imagination. He had a statue and therefore must have been a man of some stature. Beyond that, our interest failed to carry us. And it was not until my fifteenth year that I really came to know him. And then I made his acquaintance through that curious uncle of mine, who, being a perfect type of the almost completely extinct *Homo Renascencius* (or man of the Renaissance), became the chief intellectual and spiritual inspiration of my more impressionable years.

By PROFESSION my mother's brother was a physician. By inclination he also was a good musician, a painter of more than ordinary ability, a most talented linguist, an omnivorous reader, and a person of vast cultivation and wit. On the debit side I should mention that his burning curiosity about everything, however remotely connected with the human race, had used up so much of his mental and nervous energy that his last years were most sadly spent in the darkness of a completely obscured mind.

The Great War which brought about the destruction of all those decencies of life for which he had so stoutly fought during all his waking hours (and he was a very light sleeper), had probably a great deal to do with this premature prostration. But when he was in his full glory he was a godsend to a small boy who was supposed to be learning his Latin and Greek syntax by heart at the very moment when he wanted to read Vergil and Homer and who had but little respect for those grammatical irregularities which counted so heavily when the teacher took out his little gray book to write down those terrible marks which were to decide our chances of promotion.

Being blessed with all the obstinacy and plain ordinary cussedness of the race inhabiting the Low Countries by the shores of the North Sea, I was a difficult pupil. Hence six years of profound misery during which my teachers tried to push me one way while I, in all my youthful arrogance, pulled in the opposite direction. I was, of course, bound to lose out against the assembled pedagogs of a country which took its pedagogs almost as seriously as its religion, but I kept on and I will leave it to posterity to decide who was right.

The only ray of light and hope that penetrated this gloomy part of my early career came to me on Saturdays and Sundays when I could leave my exile in the good city of Ter Gouw (near which Erasmus had suffered a similar fate) and could betake myself, my week's laundry, and my unfinished Latin and Greek exercises to The Hague. Once there I would spend as much time as possible among

the books and pictures of my uncle and pick up such
crumbs of information as occasionally fell from those lips
that are now sealed forever.

It was inevitable that a humanist of the nineties of the
last century should feel a close kinship to one of the early
sixteenth. Hence Erasmus was very much in evidence.
Almost all of his works were to be found in the avuncular
library, for in those blessed days before book collecting
had become a racket, it was still possible to pick up original editions for a few stivers or quarters. Then there were
a great many engravings of the different pictures of our
famous fellow townsman. For Erasmus, who for almost
forty years of his life had been about as much in the public
eye as a modern movie star, had been the most pictorialized
figure of the first half of the sixteenth century.

The three most distinguished painters of his day had
tried their brush at him, not once but several times. Holbein, Dürer, and Quentin Matsys had done as well by him
as by any of their other customers and there are furthermore a large number of drawings, and steel and copper
engravings, which show us Erasmus engaged in his favorite and useful pastime of fishing little words out of the
cow's horn which served him as an inkstand.

The plenitude of this iconographical material (as our

modern scholars love to call it) does not indicate that
Erasmus was an inordinately vain person. As far as we
know, none of these wooden tablets graced his own walls.
Almost all his portraits had been done for the great of
this earth. Sir Thomas More is supposed to have ordered
the so-called "Paris Holbein." Another one had been in
the possession of Boniface Amerbach, the executor of
Erasmus' last will and testament (by which the good
doctor left the greater part of his considerable fortune to
be spent on scholarships for promising young men and
dowries for dutiful young women) and a third one (the
well-known long-nosed one) had been painted for the
Archbishop of Canterbury. The one I happen to like best
is the Longford Castle Holbein of the year 1523, showing
us Erasmus in his late fifties, about a dozen years before
his death. He looks delicate. His hair (or whatever there
is left of it) has turned gray and even his heavy garb of
furs seems unable to protect his shivering bones from that
feeling of cold which (together with a great many other
major and minor ailments) did so much to turn him into
one of the world's most inveterate hypochondriacs. His
thinly veined hands rest on a book. On that book two
words stand printed. They are in Greek and they are
borrowed from one of his own collections of *Adagia,* or

parables, as we would say today. They refer to his Herculean labors, as well they might!

FEW PEOPLE EVER WENT through such an immense amount of work as this indefatigable Dutchman, who with his bare hands, so to speak, undertook the problem of turning this world into a place where men and women of good will, tolerance, and mutual understanding should be able to spend their three score and ten as each other's good and well-intentioned neighbors, instead of sworn enemies. He failed, I am sorry to say, as every pioneer of a new idea is bound to fail. But enough has remained to act as a sort of leaven of our whole social and spiritual existence.

Like another curious product of the Low Countries, the venerable Baruch de Spinoza, Erasmus was able to add something to the cosmic point of view of the Western world which no oppression, repression, or coercion has ever been quite able to eradicate. It is true that neither Erasmus nor Spinoza were ever popular among the masses. This was partly their own fault. They were essentially "aristocratic" in their attitude toward life. As proud citizens of the Commonwealth of Letters, they felt that they were under the high obligation of assuming the responsibility of leadership, and as such, only the *ariston*—

the best—could ever be good enough, for even the "second best" would mean a betrayal of their duties towards their fellow men who were less well equipped to take care of themselves. They felt (as Confucius and Plato felt long before them) that if the men of the pen could influence the men of the sword, that the Pope, emperors, kings, and princes (who were in actual command of the situation), would gradually be persuaded to see what those philosophers were pleased to call "the Light" and would begin to base their efforts to rule their fellow men upon the principles of Virtue, Righteousness, and the Common Decency of Life. After that, everything would be as it should be and everybody would be prosperous and contented.

It was an admirable ideal, one that would bring about a general state of happiness which our greatly disturbed planet had never yet seen. And two and a half centuries after Erasmus' death and a hundred years after that of Spinoza, another great disciple of these two prophets from the Netherlands, one Thomas Jefferson, Esq., of Virginia, was actually to incorporate these principles into his Declaration of Independence of the United States of America.

But today we are further away from this noble prospect than ever before, unless the holocaust which is now preparing itself under our very eyes assumes such terrific proportions that the survivors will be forced to substitute reason for emotion and knowledge for prejudices. Then, at last, Desiderius Erasmus of Rotterdam, now deprived of his statue by the fury of the spiritual enemies of mankind, may have a monument in every city of this world; for then his ideas shall have become an integral part of the law of every land—and what more can we ask and hope for?

I NEED NOT BOTHER YOU about the exact date of the birth of Erasmus, for he himself was quite ignorant upon this subject. It may have been the year 1466 or 1465 or 1467. The day was October 28th, but the year will probably always remain a mystery, partly because Erasmus preferred to keep it so.

He was extremely sensitive about his doubtful status as an illegitimate child. Sometimes we have the feeling that he was rather inclined to capitalize upon his unfortunate condition. The lenient Middle Ages acknowledged and recognized bastardy as an unavoidable part of a world in which class distinctions played such a rigorous part and in which so large a number of men were condemned to a life of celibacy. The upper layers of society set the example. Emperors and princes (and even one Pope) cheerfully recognized these offspring that were born out of wedlock, and it made very little difference to King William whether he was known to his subjects as the Conqueror or the Bastard.

Erasmus, however, like all great artists, was considerable of an actor and he loved to dramatize himself. Everything that had gone wrong during the days of his early childhood, his prolonged struggle for some kind of foothold on the ladder of success, had been due, he felt, to his uncertain social standing. Even afterwards, when no person of quality felt that his home was perfect without at least one beautifully bound copy of a personal epistle, signed by the famous man, it added to his glory to know that he had reached his eminent position entirely by his own efforts and without any of the advantages of birth. "Behold me, Desiderius of Rotterdam, the most renowned scholar of the age, who yet began his career as the unknown son of an obscure father."

Psychologists inform us that all children at one time or another indulge in the pleasant luxury of considering themselves a little Oliver Twist. Erasmus was therefore only true to type when he made pathetic allusions to his having suffered all his livelong days from being a *nullius filius*. But with equal power he dramatized his endless physical sufferings, his intermittent fevers, his inability

The house in which Erasmus was born

ever to get warm enough to prevent the icy drafts from running down his spine, his susceptibility to all kinds of epidemics, the necessity of keeping his physical strength at par by just the right kind of Burgundy.

Maybe all this was true. And then, maybe he had no desire to die of such an indecorous disease as the bubonic plague or dysentery, and perhaps he really had a very genuine liking for the wines of southern France.

It is hard to come to a definite conclusion. In order to play the role he had chosen for himself, the universally acclaimed President of the Republic of Bonae Litterae, Erasmus had to create and maintain his own "act." At a very early age he decided upon the "type" for which he seemed best fitted both by nature and by his own predilections. Having chosen his role—the man of weak vitality who was nevertheless able to do the labors of ten ordinary human beings—he had to give it everything there was in him. For eighteen hours a day during more than half a century he worked to become the Edwin Booth of the Humanities and he fully succeeded in his self-appointed task. If you will make a careful study of the Dürer and Holbein pictures, painted at the moment he was at the height of his fame, you will see a man who felt rather like the cat which had eaten the canary.

It now behooves us to find out what kind of canary it was he consumed with his beloved Côte d'Or.

WE KNOW VERY LITTLE about Erasmus' father. Charles Reade pretended to know a lot. That was his right as a teller of tales, but while it makes *The Cloister and the Hearth* a first-rate novel, it does not exactly promote it to the stature of an historical book of reference. The father's name was Gerard and he was a citizen of either Rotterdam or Gouda. Those two cities were very close to each other. When we were boys, we easily covered the distance in a short day unless we were lucky and some obliging skipper gave us a lift, in which case the trip was nothing at all.

We are entirely uncertain about the man's social station and his profession. Charles Reade suggests, if I remember correctly, that he was a cleric of sorts, either a priest or some minor official of the Church. I have my doubts about the priesthood, for while a young and impetuous gentleman of the cloth may fall from grace once, he is hardly likely to repeat that mistake, which, in his own eyes and those of his superiors and neighbors, is a most heinous sin. For we know that Desiderius (the undesired Desiderius) was not the only result of his unfortunate passion. There was an elder brother named Peter for whom Desiderius felt a very sincere affection and whom he mentions more often than any of his other relatives but who remains nevertheless a shadowy figure.

As for the mother, there again are only a few definite data about any of the events in her humble existence. She was enough of a personality to arise from the anonymity that was enforced upon her by her greatly disturbed relatives and by those of the man who was the father of her children. She is said to have been a servant but there is an atmosphere about her very different from the servant-class attitude of the last half of the fifteenth century. Had she been just a household drudge, she would have been given some slight remuneration and would have been kept securely in the background until someone had been found ready to marry a young woman with two lovely little boys and a bag of ducats large enough to set her husband up in some independent little business of his own. Even when I was young, such things not only could be arranged but were quite common and ended to the complete satisfaction of all the parties involved. That she was given a household of her own and was entrusted with the education of her small sons until death took her away shows that the family on both sides had considerable confidence in her ability to take care of herself and her brood.

My own guess, based upon a fairly profound familiarity with the sort of people who were after all my own people, would be that she came from a better-middle-class background. I confess that in order to make this qualification you have to be a Dutchman with a very thorough knowledge of the set-up of our small communities where the sense of the respectable and of the practical are so closely interwoven and intertwined as to produce results totally un-understandable to an American of the twentieth century.

I see Erasmus' father as a young man who some day (if death had not prevented him) might have come into considerable property, at least from the better-middle-class point of view. He may have been a cleric, holding a small but secure position in one of the Church courts or in the management of some clerical establishment. He may have been in that hard-to-define floating position (then so common) where he was neither entirely a churchman nor entirely a secular person. In due course of time he might even have hoped to return once more to the world at large. It would then have been quite easy for him to regulate the affairs of his illegitimate offspring. All that would have been necessary was for his bride to appear at her wedding

His first skates

feaſt wearing a wide cloak or cape, hiding her young
sons. After the two of them had been declared husband
and wife, the children—thus concealed—would have been
accepted as their legitimate offspring, for during the sacred
moment when the marriage was actually declared valid,
they would have been covered by the Cloak of Chaſtity.

The Middle Ages were nothing if not practical! I like
that Cloak of Chaſtity arrangement. I wish some fashion
expert would reintroduce it into our present-day society!
It would prevent a lot of misery for totally innocent ur-
chins whose only sin consiſts in having been created without the duly ſtamped and sealed approval of the clerk of
some municipal court. But in the case of Erasmus, it was
not the Cloak of Chaſtity but the pall of death which was
draped across his family before the parents had been able
to ſtraighten out their tangled affairs. And little Gerard
Gerardszoon and Peter Gerardszoon (as their neighbors
knew the future Desiderius Erasmus and his brother)
were left to shift for themselves as beſt they could under
the tutelage of a brace of uncles who had been appointed
guardians over these unfortunate orphans and who were
obliged to make their slender inheritance go as far as they
possibly could. Probably they were not any too delighted
with the job that had been wished upon them. For (then

33

as now) it was not so easy to take full responsibility for two young boys about whom the world would always say, "Such nice children! Isn't it too bad that they were born as they were!"

AT A VERY EARLY AGE Peter and Gerard were sent to the Latin School in Gouda, not to that in Rotterdam, which may indicate that either their father was of Gouda origin or that he had relations there.

By the way, as in the rest of the story we shall speak only of Desiderius Erasmus, we might as well get that name business straightened out right here and now, for otherwise it will bother us all through this book. His father's name had been Gerardszoon which clearly indicated that the grandfather, too, had been known as Gerard. It was during this period that the world was beginning to burst through the bonds of medieval provincialism and the need was making itself felt for definite last names. These everlasting Willemszoons and Pieterszoons were making life as complicated as Norwegian and Swedish telephone books with their endless Petersens and Jensens. When Erasmus began to suspect that he was a young man with a future he cast around for a trademark suitable for the man of learning he intended to be. Since the Dutch language was still in its swaddling clothes, neither Erasmus nor his neighbors could be expected to be etymological experts. And so without the risk of being seriously contradicted he proclaimed that the name of Gerard was derived from the Dutch verb *begeren* or "to desire." Rather naïvely he connected the Dutch verb *begeren* with the Greek *eraomai* and the Latin *desiderare* and thereupon, by Latinizing them both with considerable liberty, he reached the high-sounding result of Desiderius Erasmus.

There are, I warn you, other explanations of the origin of this strange name but that is the one which seems most natural and reasonable to me. Afterwards, and probably in order to differentiate himself from other and pseudo-Erasmi (for name stealing is as old as the hills), he added the name of his home town and became Erasmus Rotterdamus, with either one or two t's. The Rotte, by the way, was the little stream which ran from the hinterland of the province of Holland (a nasty set of marshes) to that branch of the Rhine which the Dutch for some mysterious reason have always referred to as the Maas. In the year 1281 the Counts of Holland had strengthened the dykes of the Rotte, thereby making that whole region safe for permanent human habitation. And the village which thereupon arose near the dam in the Rotte became known as Rotterdam. This much for the benefit of those who, like myself, are interested in that sort of historico-geographico-philological information. And now we continue with "Henricus Rotterdamus de Erasmo Rotterdamo."

It seems that Erasmus was predestined to become an inveterate wanderer. Between his first and sixth years he moved from Rotterdam to Gouda. Next we find him still further east in Deventer. His mother apparently took him to this ancient city together with his brother. The fact that he was sent to so remote a town merely because it happened to have the best school then available is a proof that those who were entrusted with his education took their responsibilities seriously. If today you hear that a couple of children of highly irregular antecedents have been sent to the most famous prep-school in New England instead of the local high school, you feel that somebody, somewhere, is taking a personal interest in their bringing up and has thought all this out most carefully.

Their new school was conducted by those Brothers of the Common Life who ever since the middle of the fourteenth century had tried to make the Christian faith an actuality rather than a theory. Under the leadership of Geert Groote, they had founded establishments in which

His mother takes him and his brother to Deventer

both men and women deeply interested in the salvation of their souls could live in this world yet not quite of this world. Without actually taking monastic vows, these Brethren were able to spend their days pursuing their usual tasks, while keeping aloof from the temptations and tribulations of the outside world.

I don't know why, but the moment the word "common" makes its appearance in connection with a movement, that movement comes under heavy suspicion of all the "sound" members of the community, though the very term, community, is based upon the same root. For example, one of the reasons the Romans so seriously distrusted the Christians was because these pious souls shared their possessions in common with their neighbors. The cruel eradication of the Albigensians in the Middle Ages was the result of a popular crusade against their pernicious heresy of regarding all Christians as common not only in the sight of God but also in that of the dispensers of tangible treasures. The Anabaptists of the first half of the sixteenth century were no doubt a good deal of a nuisance with their cult of the nude and their other absurdities of behavior. But in order to enrage the populace against them as "enemies of society" and bring about those disgusting lynching parties which fill so many of the most disgraceful pages of the history of that disgraceful era, all the magistrates of any given city had to do was to let it be whispered about that those fiends believed in sharing the wealth in common. Luther, as soon as he heard that the rebellious peasants of northern Germany were in the habit of dividing their plunder (the wealth previously squeezed out of them by their landlords), became almost insane in the violence with which he urged the princes who were trying to suppress this revolt to eradicate this vermin from the face of the earth. And few passages in any of my books have ever caused me as much trouble as that in which I happened to say that the Pilgrims, before they reached these shores, had promised each other to share everything in common and how, during the first half dozen years of its existence, the future state of Massachusetts had been to all intents and purposes, a "communistic experiment." Yet that information was and is to be found in every serious book of American history. But people seem to become slightly uneasy the moment the harmless word "common" makes its appearance and this was just as true in the fifteenth century as it is today and apparently always has been.

The indifference of those Brethren of the Common Life towards personal possessions, the extreme simplicity of their daily lives, their insistence upon spiritual rather than worldly values—all these were regarded as indications of certain dangerous revolutionary tendencies which, if they were allowed to develop and spread, might make people so conscious of the true principles of Christianity that they might start asking questions which the rulers of the Church were by no means either ready or anxious to answer. But it was not very easy to attack or suppress these pleasant-mannered folk who lived their own lives with mouselike unobtrusiveness, who harmed no one, and who on the quiet did as much good as it was within their slender means to do. And so, provided they did not too openly indulge in the business of fishing for souls, the Brothers were as a rule left in peace. After they had gained a safe foothold among their contemporaries, they turned their attention towards the younger generation and became schoolmasters. They were soon so far ahead of all their competitors that having gone to their school in Deventer set a youngster apart, as someone who had a better chance of getting along in this world than the graduates of any other pedagogical establishment of that time.

It is therefore not quite in keeping with the facts when we dismiss the whole of Erasmus' youth as a period of undiluted suffering during which this exceedingly bright child was forever being exposed to dull-witted and pedantic disciplinarians, none of whom had any true feeling for the New Learning that was then beginning to spread across the continent of Europe. He enjoyed the teaching of some of the most remarkable men of his day. Not, it is true, for a great many years. But that has never been quite necessary. Expose normally intelligent boys and girls to an inspired teacher who can give them a real curiosity about the world they live in, and in ninety-nine cases out of a hundred they will do the rest themselves. Give them a key and show them where the lock is, and after that leave them alone. Of course, the desire to put the right keys into the right locks must be present. But that is an act of God over which we human beings have no control.

As I have said before, life for Erasmus became considerably more difficult after the death of his father and mother. Since there was no money to set the boys up in business or to start them on a career, their guardians had to fit them into some humble little niche where they might safely remain all the rest of their days without ever being in actual need. They solved their problem as might have been expected of simple Dutch people of the last quarter of the fifteenth century. It was decided that both boys should go into the priesthood. The Church asked no embarrassing questions about anyone's antecedents. The

*By temperament and inclination Erasmus was not at
all fitted for the monastic life*

Church always took care of its children. And the Church, therefore, it was to be, regardless of the personal preferences (if any) of either of the boys.

As a matter of definitely chronicled history, neither Peter nor Desiderius seems to have felt the slightest desire to become monks. But in the year 1484 young men were not asked for their opinions when it came to choosing a career and so they were shipped off, first of all to a sort of preparatory school in Bois le Duc, which Erasmus came to detest for its severity and hollow formalism, and next to the cloister of Steyn, a settlement of Augustinian monks, a short walk's distance from the city of Gouda where he had spent part of his earliest youth.

Steyn was just an average, every-day monastical establishment of the out-going Middle Ages, no better and probably no worse than the others. Erasmus came to hate the place with an all-consuming detestation. Maybe it was the food which got on his nerves. Erasmus, all his livelong days, suffered from a sort of boiled-fish phobia. I am familiar with that affliction. My own father had gone to a school in Rotterdam where twice a week (just as in the cloister Steyn) the pupils were given boiled fish and that meant that twice a week he suffered from dreadful and irrepressible attacks of seasickness. In those days, long before there was a science of child psychology, the authorities had tried to cure him of his unmistakable discomforts by forcing him to stay in the dining room regardless of his suffering. The same sort of thing may have happened to Erasmus.

He loathed the very memory of Steyn and once he had escaped from this hell on earth, he deliberately refused to return. Time and again the heads of the Augustinian order reminded him of his duty to obey the orders of his superiors and to go back to where he belonged. But the recollection of the insults and indignities which he claimed to have suffered at Steyn remained with him all through life, and his determination to find himself a career outside of the Church may well have been inspired and influenced by his absolute unwillingness ever to set foot again within those halls (and especially in that dining room) where he had spent the unhappiest years of his life.

In all fairness let it be said that other inmates of Steyn spoke quite favorably of it, that it enjoyed a reputation for its library, and that it had a more than average standing among the monasteries of the northern Netherlands of that day. And therefore, as so often happens, it may have been just a case of the wrong boy in the wrong school. But after the year 1492 all this no longer mattered. Almost exactly seven months before Columbus set foot on Cat Island, Erasmus was ordained. Two years later he somehow wangled a job as Latin secretary to a bishop in Cambrai, in northern France, a certain Hendrik van Bergen. He hastened to accept so that he might leave his place of exile and be nearer that famous University of Paris, where he some day hoped to find an opportunity to extend his classical studies to the point where he might make a real name for himself within the ranks of those who were then beginning to call themselves the Humanists—the pioneers of that new day which would see a return to glory of the old literary and artistic perfection of antiquity.

THIS GIVES ME an opportunity to define the actual part which Erasmus played on the cultural stage of his age and to draw your attention to those qualities which continue to make him and his work important for those of us who live more than four centuries after he went to his final and well-deserved rest.

From a modern point of view, Erasmus was deficient in many important qualities. He was interested in art and seems to have done a little painting of his own. The doodads with which he filled his manuscripts are not much of

43

a key to his artistic abilities but they reveal a pictorial imagination far beyond the average. He loved music and knew his way about among the composers of his time. But he had not the faintest notion about science. Nowhere among his writings do we find even the haziest reference to those unheard-of discoveries which were then occupying the minds of men and were filling them with constant wonderment at the world in which they lived. Medicine, hygiene, mathematics, astronomy, were subjects of which he seems to have been completely unaware. The social sciences, of course, had not yet been invented. No, not even remotely suspected. The poor and the rich were accepted as inevitable parts of the social organism, and few people felt the necessity of bringing about a more equitable division of the good things of this earth—except those poor heretics already mentioned, who were suppressed as soon as detected.

There were of course just as many charitably inclined people in the world then as now, but their attitude towards poverty was very much the same as the way they felt about leprosy and the plague and the other endemic diseases which gave the average human being a life-expectancy of only forty years. It was too bad this world had been arranged that way but it was the wiser and safer policy to

The city of Paris in the days of Erasmus

accept what could not be changed than to waste time in fruitless efforts at amelioration. If a person were hungry or cold, give him your old overcoat or send little Mary around with a pot of sustaining chicken broth. Nobody bothered his head to inquire into the real reason why these persons should be hungry and cold in a world which could supply of the necessities of life to everyone. But let us remember that our present economy of potential abundance would have seemed to the average citizen of the Middle Ages (accustomed as he was to an economy of insufficiency) a rather fantastic dream of an utterly impossible Utopia.

Man—when Erasmus lived—was still a beast of burden. His iron slave had not yet appeared to set him free from most of his drudgeries. Erasmus would have loved the world of today with all its conveniences and comforts (there are other parts of it he would have greatly disliked) but his approach towards a better life happened to be essentially along the lines of the prevailing Humanism. The Letters and the Arts would have to bring about a more enlightened existence, but most of all the Letters. All we have the right to ask is, "How did he behave within his own field of endeavor?" And then the answer is a clear and unequivocal: "He did a magnificent job."

THE LATIN SECRETARYSHIP to the Bishop of Cambrai (a strange job now extinct but still very much in demand in the seventeenth century when Milton made a living as Latin secretary to the Cromwellian Commonwealth) did not prove much of a success. There was too much "social life" connected with the office to satisfy a young scholar in search of enough leisure for his own studies. One could of course resign, but even the most ambitious of young literary men, ready to make the greatest of sacrifices, must eat. Only never again that dreadful fodder placed before him in old Steyn. Since that, however, might be the only other alternative unless he found himself something else right away he set to work with all his might and main to get hold of some suitable kind of employment.

It was then that Erasmus turned his hand to an art which he was to practice for a great many years to come and at which, in the end, he would acquire a proficiency that has rarely been equaled. He began to compose begging letters. But his begging letters were veritable pieces of literature. They were the exact opposite of the arrogant and ill-tempered missives with which a few hundred years later Richard Wagner would bombard those of his friends who might have a few hundred marks to spare for the future composer of *Parsifal* and the *Ring*.

I have always found it very difficult to sit in judgment on a man of genius who, as it is commonly expressed, demeans himself and degrades his profession by writing begging letters. Suppose that you know that you can write the *Meistersinger* and *Tristan und Isolde*. You have them in you, all neatly rolled up, but you need a few years during which you won't have to bother about the rent and the grocery bills to get them out of your brain and neatly put down on paper. Somebody somewhere has much more money than he needs. He likes music (or literature or painting or whatever happens to be your specialty) and he would probably be more than willing to help you out if he heard of your predicament.

Of course, Wagner, one of the worst boors of a country not exactly famous for the elegance of its manners, became absolutely intolerable the moment he set pen to paper. But fastidious Erasmus, who made as much of a fetish of good taste as of an elegant style, turned his paper prayers into such charming epistles that I am only sorry they did him so little good. As his native language expresses it so colorfully, he was forever "fishing behind the net." After

47

he had dispatched his envelope to one of his most promising "prospects," a messenger would knock at his door with the sad news that the addressee of the undelivered letter had just succumbed to the plague or to the mumps, or had lost all his money in some dangerous speculation, or had been decapitated at the behest of his loving sovereign, or had married again, or that some other calamity had overtaken him and that therefore he was from now on out of the question as a future benefactor.

Erasmus' search for the full dinner pail began, as I just told you, with that hopeful visit to the Bishop of Cambrai. There was, unfortunately, much too much social life at his court to please him. But soon His Grace was expected to set out for Rome and Erasmus was to accompany him. My Lord Hendrik van Bergen wanted to make a good showing at the Vatican and that was the real reason he had got himself such a first-class Latin secretary. And Erasmus stayed on because the chance of actually visiting the center of Christianity (and completely "found" too, instead of as a poor scholar) was not something to be taken lightly.

Suddenly the trip was called off. A friend of Erasmus, one Jacobus Badt, a distinguished citizen of the town of Bergen-op-Zoom in Brabant and a magistrate with considerable influence, suggested to the Bishop that he bestow

The road that led to Rome

an annual ſtipend upon his bright young secretary so that he might proceed to Paris and there gain an even greater proficiency in the classical tongues and become an honor to his patron. For by now it had become clear to Erasmus that, if he wanted to get anywhere at all, he muſt firſt of all learn Greek. As Greek professors were then about as scarce as good Russian teachers at our modern American universities, this was no easy undertaking. However, there was said to be a fairly competent Graecologiſt in Paris, and so off to Paris Erasmus rode and there he enrolled in the College of Montaigu.

Alas, he had gone from Scylla to Charybdis (as he would have called it in his *Adagia*) or out of the frying pan into the fire, as we say today. Compared to Montaigu, Steyn had been heaven, for Montaigu had recently been placed under the headship of a certain Jan Standonck, an ardent reformer and a leader in that "New Devotion" movement which intended to change the monaſtic eſtablishments, many of which had become sinks of iniquity, into what the clerical authorities imagined the cloiſters of a thousand years before to have been. No frivolities, no easy life, no pretext at a bit of facile scholarship, but a maximum of ſtudy and devotions with a minimum of sleep and food.

Some thirty years later, Ignatius de Loyola was also to

49

be a student at the College of Montaigu. He was not going to find anything amiss with it. That inhuman schedule of four hours of sleep, food prepared with rotten eggs (see Erasmus' letter upon those charming menus), harsh punishments—it suited him perfectly. Whereas Erasmus detested it, hated it, abhorred it, felt even sicker and weaker than usual and searched high and low that he might find some way in which to escape. For Desiderius Erasmus, in spite of his very humble antecedents, was a man of perfections, and now he found himself a "pauper student" in a college where even the richest students lived like pigs. He got infected with some horrible disease. The whole place was full of dirt. His gastric ulcers bothered him again, and every year when Lent came and the regular severity of the daily mode of life was increased by all sorts of severe self-castigations, he would fall ill, and so seriously that he was forced to go back home to Holland to recuperate with his none too hospitable relatives. His only consolation was the presence of a few congenial souls among his fellow sufferers, several of whom became his friends for life. But what a prospect, since hope of finding a really good Greek teacher had again come to naught!

And so he started in all seriousness on several volumes

Erasmus in Paris

that were out and out potboilers. Impressed by such high-sounding titles as *Adagia* (from the Classics), and Erasmus' *Colloquies,* we are apt to overlook the fact that these volumes belonged to that curious category of books which today are known to the trade as "How to" literature. The sixteenth century publishers, being just as bright as our own, had long since discovered that there were fortunes to be made out of those handy reference books which saved the average citizen the trouble of going to the original sources.

The Renaissance had made everybody conscious of the necessity of being considered a pretty good scholar. In our own commercial world, if one hopes to succeed, one must learn "how to make friends" or how to handle one's income tax. In the Year of Grace 1500, the ambitious young man who hoped to make his way must quote the Classics with ease and eloquence, must know at least ten different ways of writing a bread-and-butter letter, and must have a fitting proverb for any situation that might arise. Such volumes therefore were bound to be best sellers and that was the reason Erasmus wrote them, and while they never made him rich, they at least kept him in that decent amount of comfort which he had to enjoy if he were to function to the best of his ability.

Many people have criticized Erasmus severely for having descended to this kind of work. But why not? Did not Beethoven write the incidental music for some kind of eighteenth century movie? Was not Mozart's whole existence filled with all sorts of jobs that were done "on order" and had to be done if he hoped to keep himself and his beloved Constance out of the poor-house? And did not the great and gruff Rembrandt draw advertising pictures for an Amsterdam bookseller? Of course they did, and I think that we are very foolish to find fault with them for having undertaken such labor. For those makeshift artistic products fed them and provided them with a roof over their heads, while they prepared to do their more serious work. It is only when the potboiler becomes an end in itself that the contents are apt to smell as badly as Erasmus' boiled fish. Worse!

HERE IS ANOTHER POINT at which I ran across the tracks of Erasmus. The faithful Badt, who had been moving heaven and earth in Holland to find Erasmus some kind of employment which would give him time for his own serious studies and writings, had found him a job at last. A young and rich widowed lady, whose name was Anna van Borsselen and who was the largest landowner in Zeeland, had a son who had to be brought up. Badt had for the moment undertaken to be his teacher but the lady would soon move to her castle on the island of Noord Beveland and that was too far away from Bergen-op-Zoom. Erasmus at last saw his dream come true. His heart full of hope, he set forth to pay his respects to his Minerva of the Lowlands.

It was a very cold winter. The oldest inhabitants could not remember, etc., etc. Erasmus got as far as Veere where he was held up by a sleet storm, the worst sleet storm of a hundred years. He was in a hurry to reach the island of Noord Beveland on the other side of the Scheldt. Walking was impossible. A sleigh was out of the question. But he had to get there! So he and his *famulus* sat themselves down on their haunches on the ice and let the wind blow them across. After that, there should have been a P.S., "He got the job." But he didn't. The lady soon afterward began to interest herself in a handsome but useless young man who, attracted by her beauty and not indifferent to her riches, was quite willing to reciprocate. It was the usual story and with the usual ending. The lady, as was becoming more and more evident, was land poor. She was the owner of vast tracts of land. But that land just then could not be sold and most of the time poor Anna was unable to pay her grocer and baker. Furthermore, her own relatives and the relatives of her former husband did not at all approve of the match and were starting annoying lawsuits. In the end, Anna van Borsselen got very little and Erasmus got less—a free trip to Zeeland and a bad cold, just escaping pneumonia.

At this rate of detail, the introduction will wag the book and that should never be allowed. Anyway, I have now given you an idea of the background of our hero as a youth. Now we must let him grow into manhood.

IT WAS THE YEAR 1499 and Erasmus was therefore in his early thirties. In other words he was getting along in years and also somewhat in fame, but financially he was almost as badly off as the day he left his cloister. And the dreadful thought that he was still an Augustinian friar and one who at any moment, like a soldier on A.W.O.L., might be sent rudely back to his monastery weighed heavily upon his mind, if somewhat lightly upon his soul. For though he remained a faithful son of the Church until the end of his days, Erasmus was not really a very devout person as we understand the word. In an age when mystics were as common as buttercups in the meadows around the cloister Steyn, he had both feet firmly on the ground. The very idea of being condemned to return to his chilly prison

Erasmus crosses the ice from Veere to Noord Beveland

among the Dutch polders brought about attacks of pain in the duodenal region. There muſt be some way out and he muſt find it right away.

While in Paris he had made some extra money coaching rich young men for their examinations. One of these, a certain William Blount, afterwards Baron Mountjoy, had always urged him to pay him a visit in England. Erasmus now decided to do what he hated to do—to cross the turbulent sea which frightened the life out of him and to entruſt his delicate conſtitution to the bad food and the damp beds of the English inns about which he had already heard more than enough from his Parisian fellow ſtudents. It was the wiseſt ſtep he ever took. England—to use another classical adage—proved to be his oyſter. There at laſt he had a chance to give full vent to perhaps the moſt outſtanding of his many talents, his gifts for sociability in the trueſt and beſt sense of that pleasant and useful word.

There have been great men who did their beſt work in a sort of human vacuum, who could live quite happily and for years at a time without ever leaving the realm of their own thoughts. But there have been others—and many more of them—who needed those sparks that come from a clash between kindred souls in order to keep the fires of their enthusiasm burning. Erasmus belonged to the latter group. His own country, prosperous, smug, self-contented but preferring to exist on a basis of fat living and lean thinking, had not been able to give him that. The Bishop of Cambrai had been quite "social," but in another sense of the word than the one I mentioned a moment ago. In Paris, Erasmus' straitened circumstances had prevented him from meeting his fellow men on an equal footing. But in England he had some money in his pocket (derived from his potboilers and his activities as private tutor) and could afford his first dress suit, as we would say today. There were a large number of houses where good manners were so happily interwoven with brilliant thinking that it must have been a joy for a bright young man, starved for conversation, to find that he was given a key to the front door and bidden to make himself welcome.

That he was a Dutchman made no difference as the Middle Ages were infinitely more cosmopolitan than we are in the matter of a common culture and a common code of manners. And so Erasmus at last came into his own. At the home of Lord Mountjoy, and a few years afterward at the home of Thomas More, two of the best examples of all those virtues and graces we used to asso-

ciate with the English conception of the word "gentleman," he met everybody truly worth meeting. There was
John Colet, later Dean of St. Paul's, a dignified churchman, as sound in his learning as in his views on contem-
porary politics. There was William Lily, first headmaster
of the school founded by John Colet. There was John
Fisher, afterwards Cardinal Fisher, a man of great piety
and deep learning. There was the wife and there were the
daughters of Sir Thomas, who made his house into a place
of such simple charm and unaffected hospitality that the
guests were bound to be at their best the moment they
set foot inside the door.

Nor did it make very much difference when young
King Henry VIII first began to occupy the throne, for the
King in his own way was quite a scholar, but women, as
Sam Weller would have said, were his downfall. No sooner
had he reached the age of indiscretion than, like a lecher-
ous old hound, he only followed the tracks of his own un-
wholesome instincts and whoever opposed him was either
crushed or run underfoot. Colet died just in time to avoid
the scaffold. But Fisher and More eventually lost their
heads because of their opposition to the way in which the
King conducted his own divorce-mill. But all this was still
mercifully hidden by a distant future.

To this English period Erasmus owed that development of mind and soul which was to make him something infinitely more important than merely another clever Humanist (all the cities of the Continent were full of them) and was to turn his mind towards that new task which was to bring him the fame that ever since has been associated with his name.

AND HERE I TOUCH upon the most difficult part of my little dissertation. What, exactly, was Erasmus' new task? It was not the result of a sudden revelation, an unexpected call to duty, like that experienced by St. Paul, Mohammed, Loyola, St. Francis, and so many other great visionaries. Nor was there anything definite about the program he set himself, nor any list of achievements to be obtained like those drawn up by Benjamin Franklin or Mr. Kipps. On the contrary, it was all so vague that Erasmus, even on his deathbed, could not possibly have told his best friend what he had tried to achieve. And more than three centuries have had to go by before we have begun to understand what he was trying to accomplish, and so paint for ourselves a clear picture of the new world he hoped to recreate among the ruins of the old one.

Let us remember that Erasmus like ourselves lived in

Erasmus goes to England

an era when an old world, an old form of society, an old culture, was slowly disappearing from view while the new one had not yet made its appearance with sufficient clarity to allow anyone to predict its shape, color, and inner substance. Erasmus, therefore (and very much like ourselves), was doomed to spend his days in an age of uncertainty and of doubt, when all the old values were being revaluated into new ones and when the verities of today might be exposed as the falsehoods of tomorrow. For feudalism was dead or dying and a new class of people were appearing upon the scene to take the place of the old masters.

That was the class to which we usually refer as the middle class, but that word is not going to help me much in trying to explain the role which Erasmus was able to play. When we use the expression "middle classes," we unconsciously think of neat little suburban houses with commuting husbands and pleasant wives who run the home and see to it that the children get to school on time. The Dutch word *burgher* not only implied all that but a lot more. The burgher had gradually worked himself out of very humble beginnings into a creature who occupied a place that was neither peasant nor noble but that stood right in between these two extremes. Since we have never recognized the existence of these extremes as established and accepted subdivisions of our own social order, it is almost impossible for us to realize what it must have meant to the people of the Middle Ages to watch the rise of this new social layer which no longer depended upon the ownership of land for its wealth, but which through its accumulated riches could safely defy king and baron and which in the end could even successfully defy the power of the Church.

Few countries had undergone that change as early or as completely as the Netherlands. The Low Countries had somehow been spared those endless and futile wars between powerful families which had played such havoc in France and England. Their remoteness and poverty and their sudden and unexpected rise to wealth had prevented the growth of those powerful medieval clans which had exercised a complete domination over the social, political, and economic development of other parts of Europe. And now, when the whole planet was suddenly being opened up to the white man's exploitation and the North Sea was taking the place of the Mediterranean as the center of wealth and enterprise, they were gathering a golden harvest.

They had been accumulating a certain amount of money ever since a bright fisherman in Zeeland discovered a method of preserving the humble herring so that it could be turned into an article of export. The medieval world with its many faſt days had proven a moſt lucrative market for this new addition to its daily fare. These profits from the herring business were now available to build the bigger ships necessary for the overseas trade, and already in the days of Erasmus the river cities of the Low Countries with their easy access to the North Sea and the Baltic and the Arctic and the Atlantic oceans were way ahead of their rivals in Germany, France, and England in the matter of a fairly well-divided prosperity, and it was in these cities that Erasmus had spent the impres, sionable years of his youth.

THE WRITERS of Utopias and those philosophers who have meditated upon the Ideal Form of Government have always been inspired by some concrete example of government, with which they themselves were familiar. They had of course idealized their model. Look at Plato's *Republic*! What was it but the perfection of the old Athenian commonwealth? What was the *City of God* of St. Augustine but imperial Rome on a divine basis? And Sir Thomas More's *Utopia* is not some fanciful image hanging in the air, but like Bacon's *New Atlantis* it represents what these authors imagined England might have been if it had been ruled on a basis of justice and enlightenment.

Erasmus never gave us a description of his own ideal state but he worked for it harder than almost any other man. And his Perfect Commonwealth (could it have been otherwise?) was a small Dutch town of the latter half of the fifteenth century, but improved to the nth degree. I know that in referring to his native land Erasmus rarely has a pleasant thing to say. The people were coarse. He did not like the way they built their houses and detested the food they ate. He regretted their lack of manners and thought of them as being so earthy that he could never hope to live among them and be truly happy. In speaking this way about his compatriots he was partly living up to an old and well-known habit of the Dutch who dearly love to denounce everything connected with their fatherland. This was common (and still is) among all the members of small nations. Norwegians, Danes, Swedes, and Swiss spend about half their time abroad telling each other and whosoever cares to listen what dreadful countries

His perfect commonwealth was a small Dutch town

they hail from. But when something happens to that greatly despised homeland (as it happened last year when they were overrun by the Nazis), they will give their last penny and their last ounce of strength to set the old soil free from its unwelcome visitation.

This eternal faultfinding therefore meant nothing at all, and let it be confessed that Erasmus was perfectly right in a great many of his other accusations. During the Middle Ages, the Low Countries had been so far removed from the real center of civilization as to be comparatively forgotten. There was no Dutch court in the actual sense of the word until the year 1813 and the absence of such an institution made itself felt in the absence of those "courtly" manners which Erasmus could have observed (though at first only from a distance) in Brussels, Paris, and London, and in the rich towns of Flanders, which for a long time had been under the domination of the Dukes of Burgundy, the most civilized *grands seigneurs* of the out-going Middle Ages, with their sincere love for art and music and everything else that could add a colorful pattern to their official existence.

Nor had that part of the Low Countries where Erasmus was born ever favored the development of that special class of minor feudal nobles who had played such a prominent part in the life of central Europe. On every side he had been surrounded by a solid "burgherdom." I am sorry that I must use this word again, but there is no really good equivalent for it in our American tongue. It is true, the French Revolution made us conscious of the term *bourgeoisie,* but *burgherdom* was something else again. It was a kind of *bourgeoisie* which had escaped so recently from its own inferior position that it was still fully conscious of its duties and obligations towards the community at large. As a result, most of those small cities were exceedingly well administered. There were as yet few traces of that peculiar democracy which we have come to consider as the beginning and the end of all true happiness. The *demos,* the great mass of the people, were still far removed from any direct participation in the conduct of affairs. But the leaders of the underprivileged who were bright enough to have worked their way up from the ranks, had many opportunities to make their influence felt. And so the Low Countries were far ahead of the rest of the world in the way in which the people had become masters of their own fate. And this new development was beginning to show itself in the greatly increased well-being of all those who had found a new freedom behind the walls of their small settlements among the marshes of the North and Zuyder Seas.

Those towns, for example, were kept comparatively clean. They made provisions for the sick and the poor and they took excellent care of their orphans. Their charity as well as their medical conceptions may not have been based upon a scientific conception of the problems of poverty and disease. But if one caught leprosy, there was a place where he could go. And if one had grown too old to work, there was a home which, as all those who have ever visited the Frans Hals Museum in Haarlem will remember, was something very different from one of Charles Dickens' workhouses. It was a place where one could be old and poor and the object of public charity without losing that modicum of self-respect which is the last remnant of happiness of the disinherited of this earth.

As for the children, they were still considered to be an element in society which should be seen (not too much) but not heard. But they had become a subject of serious consideration to the new guardians of the public welfare. They were not exactly encouraged to strive after achievements beyond their natural station in life, but they were most carefully trained for the humbler activities in which they were supposed to spend their days on earth.

And while few of them went in for reading the *belles lettres* of their day, almost all of them were able to spell at least their own names on the few occasions when that was absolutely necessary.

As for the physical aspects of those cities, the little that remains shows us that the men who supervised the municipal architecture had long since realized that one could not hope to bring up people with well-balanced minds among surroundings that were the very negation of human decency. It is true that all this was done "for" the people rather than "by" the people, except in an indirect way. But just the same, the results were something acceptable "to" all the people and it was not until many centuries later, when this form of government had become petrified (as every form of government will in due course of time), that there was a demand for something different.

Erasmus was the direct and immediate product of that kind of middle class culture. And some of it stuck to him all through his life.

THEN—something else we should remember—those people of the North, who lived far removed from the luxuries of the Southland, had remained on the whole as simple in their religious concepts as in their notions about their daily

The luxuries of the Southland

existence. The more objectionable symptoms of spiritual disintegration which had already become so very noticeable nearer to the Holy See had not yet made their appearance in the world in which Erasmus spent his childhood days. Undoubtedly much was wrong with the Church as Erasmus knew it when he was a boy; but conditions had not yet passed beyond the point of redemption. So it was still possible (as he and his neighbors felt) to bring about the necessary reforms without tearing down the entire edifice and the people felt convinced that they could institute the necessary changes if only they were left to themselves and were allowed to follow the guidance of their own common sense.

Having been brought up in comparative liberty, they strongly resented all undue influence on the part of the authorities, especially if these authorities happened to be foreigners. For the burghers of Erasmus' day were completely provincial in everything pertaining to their own daily habits, customs, and prejudices. They considered a man who lived only a few miles away a foreigner. I hardly need stress what they thought of those Spaniards and Italians who were then beginning to snoop around among them for possible whiffs of heresy. They just did not want them around. If any dangerous doctrines in their own communities were to be detected, they themselves intended to be the detectors, but no interference by any outsiders, *if you please*!

Erasmus therefore knew that reasonably well-governed communities were an actual possibility. All one needed was a certain amount of intelligence, honesty, and a willingness to live and let live. There was, of course, that lack of polish and elegance, of courtly manners and of agreeable conversation among these crude fishermen and tradespeople which made it difficult for one to whom these qualities meant so much to live contentedly among them. But if those pleasant extras could be added to the substructure of the prevailing forms of government, one would have a world which, so Erasmus thought, would be a decided improvement upon the old one. And he seems to have been convinced that it would not be beyond the limit of possibility to bring this state of affairs about by merging the culture of classical times with the sound virtues of the Christian Church, as they had originally been preached unto the disciples of Christ himself.

I fear that I am putting all this rather crudely, but I rather think that if I had had a chance to discuss all this with Erasmus over a glass of Côte d'Or, he might have confessed that something like that was actually in his mind when he started upon those labors which were to keep him busy during the last half of his life and which led to what the world has, since then, accepted as the Erasmian philosophy.

Unlike the system of Spinoza (who was nevertheless greatly influenced by Erasmus), there was nothing definite or mathematical about it. His ideas lay spread throughout all sorts and kinds of literary products, from collections of classical proverbs to handbooks on literary etiquette and devotional exercises, which in his case are exercises in common sense rather than theology.

It is perhaps unfortunate that Erasmus did not make his appearance a half century earlier or later than he did, but such things cannot be helped and vain regrets are as useless in history as they are in life. Given the circumstances under which he was forced to live, we must, I think, confess that by and large he did about as well as one could have expected of a person of his mental and physical make-up.

During the beginning of his life he fought the abuses which during the last thousand years had developed inside of the Church. Then Martin Luther made his appearance with his uncompromising insistence that the necessary changes be brought about right then and there.

Erasmus, the ardent champion of a universal culture, fore-
saw very clearly what Luther's activities must lead to and
that they might destroy that noble edifice in which all good
Christians had found a common home.

After that, there was but one course open to him. He
must do his best to counteract the influence of Luther. A
modern scholar with an original turn of mind has recently
pointed out that Erasmus, the sound Dutch burgher, could
never have had anything in common with the German
peasant, Luther. I think, on the whole, that he has come
nearer to the truth than any other writer who has devoted
his attention to this subject. Just as Jefferson, the Virginian,
could never have really cooperated with the New England
Adamses upon a basis of cordial understanding, so Erasmus and Luther were bound to dislike each other. They
breathed the same air and they lived at the same time.
They spoke almost the same language and, in the eyes of
the superficial observer, they fought in the same cause.
But they looked differently; they dressed differently; they
ate differently; they laughed at a different kind of joke.
They enjoyed different kinds of food, and the wine that
was nectar to one was poison to the other. When going
forth to combat they preferred to use different kinds of
weapons, and in their heart of hearts, they detested each

Erasmus arrives in Venice

other as cordially as if they had been enemies instead of potential allies. And, therefore, they could never really hope to understand or appreciate each other, for one of them was a Dutch burgher and the other, a German peasant.

IN THE YEAR 1505 when Erasmus was visiting Lord Mountjoy for the second time, he got his chance, at last, to visit Rome. Baptista Boerio, the King's private physician, asked him to go to Italy as the tutor of his two young sons, about to undertake that "grand voyage" which was then a necessary part of the education of all young men of good family.

First of all, the three of them, together with their servants and letters of credit, went to Turin, where Erasmus got his Ph.D. From there they proceeded to Bologna where they spent a full year at the local university. Then the Boerio boys returned to England while Erasmus used the money he had earned to proceed to Venice, where Aldus Manutius, the most distinguished printer of that day, had undertaken to publish a new and very superior edition of his *Adagia,* those classical proverbs, the number of which he had now increased from a mere eight hundred to more than three thousand.

Next he went to Padua where he met another pupil, one Alexander Stewart, the illegitimate son of James IV of Scotland. Together with this young man he now went to Siena and next to Rome. There Erasmus was received with great honor. His writings had already spread his fame as the foremost Latin stylist of his day and the Vatican, already fighting its first battles against the forces of Reform, felt that it might derive great benefits from this highly accomplished cleric who could handle his goose-quill as if it had been a steel rapier but who, at the same time, was able to make a friend of the enemy he had just disarmed.

Erasmus was made to understand that if he would remain at the Papal Court, he could, so to speak, write his own check for the future. Alexander Stewart, his young charge, had suddenly been called back to Scotland and Erasmus was therefore free to go or to stay. He carefully weighed all the pros and cons. If he stayed on in Rome, he would never again have to worry about his daily bread and cheese. He also would have the best libraries in the Christian world at his disposal. But he would lose that which he valued most of all—his freedom of thought and action. He would be obliged to take sides and must leave the "middle of the road" which he preferred to follow.

72

Erasmus crosses the Alps

He drew up his balance sheet with painstaking care. When he came to the conclusion that his personal liberty of action meant more to him than anything else, he expressed his profound gratitude to his kind and well-intentioned protectors, and departed for England.

His road led northward through those dreadful mountains which filled the people of the Middle Ages with about the same horror as Death Valley did our own pioneers of a hundred years ago. He was by now sufficiently well-to-do to travel like a gentleman. He could afford three horses, one for himself and one for his servant, and one for his books and his inevitable supply of the good wine from Burgundy. As the horses knew much better where to go than their riders, the passengers had a lot of time in which to think for themselves. By fully occupying his mind, Erasmus might even avoid seeing those terrible pinnacles which at any moment threatened to crush him, and those chasms which yawned at him from every side.

But Erasmus was neither snapped at by a pinnacle nor yawned at by a chasm and, after an uneventful voyage by way of Constance, Strasburg, and Antwerp, he safely reached London. He told his host, Sir Thomas More, that during his trip across the Alps he had thought of making

73

some sort of contribution towards the so-called "Fool Literature" of that day and that he intended to do this by writing a booklet in praise of folly. It would bear the title of *Moriae Encomium,* this being a pun on the name of Sir Thomas.

There is nothing surprising in this. Erasmus, like all literary men of his age, was an incorrigible punster. As he had learned his Latin out of grammars which were chiefly composed of innocuous little riddles, he had had a good training for this sort of work. And as for his appeal to the Goddess of Folly, that too was entirely in keeping with the literary pattern of both the Middle Ages and the Renaissance.

Frontal attacks against the established order of things were, of course, out of the question. But for many hundreds of years there had been one class of people who had been privileged to speak their own mind, regardless of consequences, and who, even at the courts of emperors and kings, had been permitted to give utterance to ideas and theories totally at variance with those held by their masters. I refer to the so-called court fools. Originally they had been dwarfs and human monsters, kept around the premises to amuse the guests by their queer antics. Gradually there had arisen a definite class of professional "fools" whose business it was to divert their employers from their mighty affairs of State by entertaining them with remarks which today would be considered much too rough-and-ready for the taSte of cultivated ladies and gentlemen. But the Middle Ages and the Renaissance were very plain-spoken and even some of the puns of the Immortal William would not be tolerated in our textbooks if our eminent professors who edit those volumes realized what they really meant.

Charles I was the laSt English monarch to avail himself of the services of an official court fool, but the inStitution as such survived for many more centuries, only it moved from the royal courts to the circus. Half a century ago when I was young, a clever clown with a gift for quick repartee and a salty wit was Still beyond the law when it came to the criticism of public affairs. Forty years ago I remember an occasion in St. Petersburg when the capital of CzariSt Russia was being moSt sadly adminiStered by a gentleman whose name in the tongues of the WeSt meant "Bigger." A clown appeared one evening in the ring of a visiting circus dragging two hogs behind him. "Look at these," he said. "This swine is big but this one is Bigger." EnthusiaStic applause showed that the public had got the meaning, but even the all-powerful police of the Little

Father dared not go against tradition. The clown was warned not to be quite so funny the next night but he was not molested. And only a short while ago, the beloved Fratellinis of Paris could regale the multitudes with a little bull fight of their own which was one of the most pungent lampoons upon the last king of Spain I was ever fortunate enough to witness.

All that held true of Europe. On this side of the ocean the useful functions of the court fools as critics-at-large were for a great many years continued by our columnists. Unfortunately that sort of buffoonery, in order to be entirely successful, has to be rather local. As soon as the columnists got to boiler-plating their witty cogitations and observations, they began to lose in influence. Today the ancient and honorable guild of the professional jesters has become almost as extinct as that of the diplomatists of the school of Disraeli and Bismarck. May they rest in peace, for while they lived, they fulfilled a very useful function in the lives of nations. They acted as a kind of verbal safety valve through which the pent-up steam of popular resentment and criticism could find a means of escape. Those safety valves are now gone. Hence, to a much greater extent than most people suspect, those endless explosions which shake our poor earth.

Erasmus' method of working while dictating to a secretary

THE PRAISE OF FOLLY

When Erasmus was born, the "fool literature" to which I have just referred was enjoying great popularity. In the year 1509, when he first conceived the idea of writing his treatise, *The Praise of Folly,* there were already two English translations of Sebastian Brant's famous *Narrenschiff* or *Ship of Fools,* in which not less than a hundred and twenty-two different kinds of fools had been carefully enumerated and described. The original German version had been published in the year 1494. Although (for the sake of greater safety) it had been written in the author's rather obscure Swabian dialect, it had been welcomed by the learned and clerical worlds as a "divine satire" and its success had been so great that Brant's *Grete Shyppe of Fooles,* which had carried only masculine passengers, was shortly afterwards followed by no fewer than six vessels filled to the gunwales with foolish females.

Then as now, the stealing of another person's literary inventions was not considered a very serious crime and Shyppes of Fooles bearing all kinds of flags were soon navigating the seas of public approval. Erasmus therefore was not guilty of a really novel idea when he wrote his own *Praise of Folly*. Only he was so much cleverer and so much more entertaining a writer than his rivals that his foolish outpourings have survived whereas the con-

77

tributions of the others have long since been forgotten or at best are examined by those unfortunate young men and young women who have to know the literature of that period for their eagerly sought Ph.D.

JUST BECAUSE Erasmus had thought of composing such an *opusculum* while crossing the Alps, it did not mean that he would necessarily write it. Every author has at least a dozen ideas a day and many of them are excellent, but the mortality among these "sudden ideas" is almost as great as that among our domestic shrimps (99½% and if ever it should grow less, all the oceans would gradually be turned into solid layers of shrimps). And Erasmus might never have put his nonsense to paper if it had not been for a slight illness which forced him to take to his bed as soon as he had reached Thomas More's cozy and warm residence in Bucklersbury.

In a letter dated from Antwerp some six years later, he tells us all about the incident:

"I was staying with More after my return from Italy and I was kept several days in the house by an attack of lumbago. My books had not yet arrived and even if they had, my illness forbade exertion in more serious studies. So, in order to have something to do, I began to amuse myself with *The Praise of Folly,* not with the intention of publishing the result but to relieve the discomfort of sickness by this sort of distraction. I showed a specimen of the unfinished work to some of my friends in order to heighten the enjoyment of all this ridiculousness by sharing it. They were mightily pleased and insisted upon my going on. I complied and spent some seven days upon the work, an expenditure of time which I thought out of proportion to the importance of the subject. Afterwards the same persons who had encouraged me to write contrived to have the book taken to France and have it printed, but from a copy not only faulty but also incomplete. The failure of the work to please the public was clearly indicated by its being reprinted more than seven times in a few months and that in different places. I wondered myself what people really found to like in it."

This letter, as the reader will easily understand, was a mere smoke-screen. Erasmus never denied being the author of *The Praise of Folly.* But he was a timid soul when he was faced by the prospect of the torture chamber and the faggot, so he did not exactly stress his authorship of this little "Critical Study of the Times." He just laughed it off as something he might perhaps have jotted down for his own amusement, when he had nothing better to do.

Whereas among those who understood him and were his friends, he gave quite a different and more direct answer. Nor could he very well have done otherwise. For it was he himself who had taken his manuscript to Paris during a brief visit he seems to have paid the French capital in the month of April of the year 1511.

This period of his life is the most obscure one, about which we know practically nothing, but it was a time of great inner development. Under the influence of his English friends, Sir Thomas, John Colet, and Bishop Fisher, he was at last beginning to turn towards the serious part of his career and was working diligently on his improved edition of the New Testament and on those letters of Jerome, which (as he hoped) were to make it possible for the public at large to become directly acquainted with the true literary beginnings of the Christian faith. He must have worked very hard and cannot have gone out in society very much, for he almost completely disappears from view for more than a year and a half. There are indications that he took a lively and direct interest in the educational plan of John Colet and even helped him with his project to take the schools out of the hands of the Church and the rich men and women who had founded private colleges and to turn them into public institutions.

*Erasmus spends the last year with his publisher
Froben in Basel*

All this changed after the year 1514, in which he had moved to Basel that he might be near his publisher, Johann Froben, that well-known graduate of Basel University who had given up an academic career to turn printer. Then too we hear of certain reactions to his *Praise of Folly*.

In this book, as you will soon find out for yourselves, Erasmus hardly ever appears in person. It is the Goddess of Folly who is the actual heroine and who does the real talking. At first she is only the Laughing Deity, addressing the multitudes from her cathedra while the famous Dr. Erasmus sits modestly on the steps of this wooden contraption and does a little quiet prompting. But gradually the lady changes her mode of attack. She turns from an amiable and light-hearted commentator into a stern-faced female Jeremiah who bewails the lack of sense among the poor mortals who have gathered together to listen to her exhortations. Then she once more returns to her original method of approach and indulges in a broad kind of satire in which she proves that even wise King Solomon and the Apostle Paul have occasionally sung the praises of the Goddess of Folly.

To bring about this unexpected conclusion, Erasmus was obliged to twist several Biblical passages in a way which will seem quite outrageous to a modern generation

which is no longer in the habit of taking religion as completely for granted as the people of the sixteenth century
used to do. They thought it quite natural that John Colet
should restrict the number of pupils admitted to his
famous school to 153 because that happened to be the number of the miraculous draught of fishes. The very idea of
making one of the Apostles take an active part in a pro-
cession of fools is apt at first to shock us as something that
should not even be suggested. But the contemporaries of
Erasmus seem to have taken his observations and criti-
cisms as much for granted as we ourselves do when we go
to the theater and watch our economic and social systems
being taken completely apart and then thrown upon the
scrap-heap. And not only did Erasmus escape all unhappy consequences from his bitter attack upon the official world of his day, but those who praised his work vastly
outnumbered those who disapproved of it.

The Pope, no one less than the formidable Julius II, the
Italian prince who laid the first plans for the new church
of St. Peter, the founder of the Vatican museum and a
great personal friend of Raphael, Bramante, and Michel-
angelo, and a strong and bold and wise ruler, was not the
sort of person to have taken any ordinary kind of per-

sonal insult with a meek turning of the other cheek. But in a letter which Erasmus wrote in the beginning of the year 1518 (five years after the death of Julius) he informs his correspondent: "His Holiness read the *Moriae* in person but he laughed. His only comment was, 'I am glad that our Erasmus himself is in the book.' And yet, I confess I have dealt with no other people more harshly than with the Popes."

As for his successor, Leo X (born Giovanni de' Medici and again not the sort of person to take an attack upon his office lightly), we know from a letter written by the Abbot of St. Bertin's at St. Omer in France that Erasmus' *opusculum* had not only pleased the whole learned world but also the bishops, archbishops, kings, cardinals, and even His Holiness, who had read the whole of it from beginning to end with evident delight.

THERE WERE, OF COURSE, others who took a less lenient view of this roughshod charge upon all they held sacred. From the University of Louvain, as might have been expected in view of its reputation for bigotry and rustic narrow-mindedness, came a few feeble objections. One young teacher, fresh from the plow and bearing the appropriate name of Dorp, undertook to castigate the great Humanist for having dared to treat of holy matters with such undue levity and asked him to refrain—if for nothing else, at least for his own reputation. "Formerly," so he warned him, "everyone admired your writings . . . but this wretched *Moriae* is upsetting everything."

Twenty years later a Spanish divine offered a somewhat different kind of criticism. "Erasmus," he wrote, "in the guise of a jester is destroying the whole Church with his quips and jokes." In this he was mistaken. The Church not only survived but gained a much greater inner strength. *The Praise of Folly,* however, drew public attention to a great many abuses which might one day lead to a most deplorable schism. That innocent-looking little bundle of good-natured pleasantries and humorous fancies was in reality a tiny barrel full of that dangerous explosive known as saltpeter, which was then beginning to be called gunpowder.

Who finally caused the detonation that rent asunder that ancient edifice of a common faith, it is difficult to state. There were too many people engaged in the task of destruction and reconstruction to pick a single name. But let it be said in defense of Erasmus that he had boldly inscribed his name upon his little package of combustibles, that he had not hidden it in some obscure cellar but had

Busy till the very last

placed it in full view of all those who had eyes to see. He had even placed a red flag of warning right beside it and a placard bearing the words: *Danger! Ideas at work!*

ERASMUS lived long enough to welcome more than forty editions of his *Praise of Folly*. Nor did he have to wait long for his foreign translations. The first of these, a French one, appeared in 1517. Then in rapid succession came others in German, Dutch, Flemish, and English. After that they rattled merrily from the presses until the masses could listen to the sermon of the great Goddess of Folly in Swedish, Danish, Polish, Russian, Czech, and Greek. In the year 1842 even Spain followed suit and after that the people who had given the world the greatest story about human folly could also read this product of the councilor and teacher of their mighty King Charles, known to the rest of the world as the great Emperor Charles V.

Some of those editions and translations were entirely legitimate. Others were stolen. But the fact that publishers were willing to go to the trouble of pilfering this work shows how great the popular demand was for a kind of literary product that as a rule had been so much caviar to the multitudes. The first English translation, as far as I know, appeared in the year 1549 and there have been a great many others since. One by Professor Hoyt Hopewell Hudson of Princeton was published only the other day, but unfortunately too late to be of any guidance to us.

We ourselves have used the translation of one John Wilson, a lawyer and playwright who was born in the year 1627 and died in the year 1696. He was not a radical but, on the contrary, a most ardent royalist who got a lucrative political job in Ireland because he happened to be a crony of the Duke of York. He wrote in the vernacular of his day, but we have not changed it much, except that we have introduced subheads to make it easier for the reader to follow Dame Folly while she holds forth upon her favorite subject. As for the translation by Wilson, we chose it because in his revaluation of the original Latin he seems to have caught a great deal of the liveliness and vigor of the Erasmian text itself. As for stuffing the book full of learned notes, we thought of it but gave the idea up. It might have caused the reader to feel the same resentment as he did when he was forced to work his way through *Hamlet* or *Macbeth* so completely buried beneath notes, annotations, connotations, and explanations that the play ceased to be the thing and the erudition of the professor became the real center of interest.

For that same reason, I shall now bid you farewell.

Erasmus Rotterdamus is the real hero of this volume and not his humble admirer and pupil,

Henricus Rotterodamus.

A short P. S. about the illustrations. The book was in such popular demand that Froben soon thought of bringing out an illustrated edition. The famous Hans Holbein had apparently given the publisher the idea by scribbling sketches of the different scenes in a copy of the book which he had received as a present. We might have used these illustrations for our own edition, but it seemed so much fun to do them again in a somewhat more up-to-date manner that I asked permission to play Holbein to this modern version of the work of my beloved fellow townsman.

I am the owner of a totally unknown portrait of Erasmus in oil which cannot be much older than a century or at most a century and a quarter. People who know about such things suspect it to be a copy of a Flemish original which has disappeared. Anyway, it is some kind of direct link with my revered master and I am very proud to possess it. Every evening after I had finished a new batch of pictures, I used to place them on the bookshelf right underneath the image of the learned Desiderius. One day when unexpectedly I came into the room, I found the old gentleman smiling at the sketches right beneath him. That was the most welcome reward I could ever hope or expect to receive for any of my modest labors in the realm of the arts.

And so—

Valete, carissimi carissimaeque, ac favere mihi pergite.

H. R.

Wednesday, January 14, 1942.
Nieuw Veere
Old Greenwich, Connecticut

Erasmus of Rotterdam
To his Friend Thomas More, Health:

AS I WAS coming awhile since out of Italy for England, that I might not waste all that time I was to sit on Horsback in foolish and illiterate Fables, I chose rather one while to revolve with my self something of our common Studies, and other while to enjoy the remembrance of my Friends, of whom I left here some no lesse learned than pleasant. Amongst these you, my More, came first in my mind, whose memory, though absent your self, gives me such delight in my absence, as when present with you I ever found in your company; than which, let me perish if in all my life I ever met with any thing more delectable. And therefore, being satis-

91

fy'd that something was to be done, and that that time was no wise proper for any serious matter, I resolv'd to make some sport with The Praise of Folly.

But who the Devil put that in thy head ? you'l say. The first thing was your sirname of More, which comes so near the word *Moriæ* (Folly) as you are far from the thing. And that you are so, all the world will clear you. In the next place, I conceiv'd this exercise of wit would not be least approv'd by you ; inasmuch as you are wont to be delighted with such kind of mirth, that is to say, neither unlearned, if I am not mistaken, nor altogether insipid, and in the whole course of your life have play'd the part of a Democritus. And though such is the excellence of your Judgement that 'twas ever contrary to that of the people's, yet such is your incredible affability and sweetness of temper that you both can and delight to carry your self to all men a man of all hours.

Wherefore you will not only with good will accept this small Declamation, but take upon you the defence of 't, forasmuch as being dedicated to you, it is now no longer mine but yours. But perhaps there will not be wanting some wranglers that may cavil and charge me, partly that these toyes are lighter than may become a Divine, and partly more biting than may beseem the modesty of a

Christian, and consequently exclaim that I resemble the Antient Comedy, or another Lucian, and snarle at every thing. But I would have them whom the lightness or foolery of the Argument may offend, to consider that mine is not the first of this kind, but the same thing that has been often practis'd even by great Authors : when Homer, so many Ages since, did the like with the battel of Frogs and Mice ; Virgil, with the Gnat, and Puddings ; Ovid, with the Nut ; when Polycrates, and his Corrector Isocrates, extol'd Tyranny ; Glauco, Injustice ; Favorinus, Deformity, and the quartan Ague ; Synescius, Baldness ; Lucian, the Fly, and Flattery ; when Seneca made such sport with Claudius's Canonizations ; Plutarch, with his Dialogue between Ulysses and Gryllus ; Lucian and Apuleius, with the Asse ; and some other, I know not who, with the Hog that made his last Will and Testament, of which also even S. Jerome makes mention.

And therefore if they please, let 'em suppose I play'd at Tables for my diversion, or if they had rather have it so, that I rod on a Hobby-horse. For what injustice is it, that when we allow every course of life its Recreation, that Study only should have none ? especially when such toyes are not without their serious matter, and foolery is so handled that the Reader that is not altogether thick-skull'd may reap more benefit from 't than from some men's crabbish and specious Arguments. As when one, with long study and great pains, patches many pieces together on the praise of Rhetorick or Philosophy ; another makes a Panegyrick to a Prince ; another encourages him to a War against the Turks ; another tells you what will become of the world after himself is dead ; and another finds out some new device for the better ordering of Goat's-wooll : for as nothing is more trifling than to treat of serious matters triflingly, so nothing carries a better grace, than so to discourse of trifles as a man may seem to have intended them least. For my own part, let other men judge of what I have written ; though yet, unlesse an overweening opinion of my self may have made me blind in my own cause, I have prais'd Folly, but not altogether foolishly.

And now to say somewhat to that other cavil, of biting. This liberty was ever permitted to all men's wits, to make their smart witty reflections on the common errors of mankind, and that too without offence, as long as this liberty does not run into licentiousness ; which makes me the more admire the tender ears of the men of this age, that can away with solemn Titles. Nay, you'l meet with some so preposterously religious, that they will sooner endure the broadest scoffs even against Christ himself,

than hear the Pope or a Prince be toucht in the least, especially if it be any thing that concerns their profit ; whereas
he that so taxes the lives of men, without naming any
one in particular, whither, I pray, may he be said to bite,
or rather to teach and admonish ? Or otherwise, I beseech
ye, under how many notions do I tax my self ? Besides,
he that spares no sort of men cannot be said to be angry
with any one in particular, but the vices of all.

And therefore, if there shall happen to be any one that
shall say he is hit, he will but discover either his guilt or
fear. Saint Jerome sported in this kind with more freedome
and greater sharpnesse, not sparing sometimes men's very
name. But I, besides that I have wholly avoided it, I have
so moderated my stile, that the understanding Reader will
easily perceive my endeavours herein were rather to make
mirth than bite. Nor have I, after the Example of Juvenal,
raked up that forgotten sink of filth and ribaldry, but laid
before you things rather ridiculous than dishonest.

And now, if there be any one that is yet dissatisfied,
let him at least remember that it is no dishonour to be
discommended by Folly ; and having brought her in speaking, it was but fit that I kept up the character of the person. But why do I run over these things to you, a person
so excellent an Advocate that no man better defends his

Client, though the cause many times be none of the beſt ?
Farewell, my beſt disputant More, and ſtoutly defend
your Moriæ.

*From the Country,
the 5th of the Ides of June*

An Oration, of feigned matter,
spoken by Folly in her own Person

AT WHAT RATE soever the World talks of me
(for I am not ignorant what an ill report Folly
hath got, even amongſt the moſt Foolish), yet
that I am that She, that onely She, whose Deity recreates
both gods and men, even this is a sufficient Argument,
that I no sooner ſtept up to speak to this full Assembly,
than all your faces put on a kind of new and unwonted
pleasantness. So suddenly have you clear'd your brows,
and with so frolique and hearty a laughter given me your
applause, that in troth, as many of you as I behold on
every side of me, seem to me no less than Homer's gods
drunk with Nectar and Nepenthe ; whereas before, ye

sat as lumpish and pensive as if ye had come from consulting an Oracle. And as it usually happens when the Sun begins to shew his Beams, or when after a sharp Winter the Spring breathes afresh on the Earth, all things immediately get a new face, new colour, and recover as it were a certain kind of youth again : in like manner, by but beholding me, ye have in an inſtant gotten another kind of Countenance ; and so what the otherwise great Rhetoricians with their tedious and long-ſtudied Orations can hardly effect, to wit, to remove the trouble of the Mind, I have done it at once, with my single look.

But if ye ask me why I appear before you in this ſtrange dress, be pleas'd to lend me your ears, and I'le tell you ; not those ears, I mean, ye carry to Church, but abroad with ye, such as ye are wont to prick up to Jugglers, Fools and Buffons, and such as our Friend Midas once gave to Pan. For I am dispos'd awhile to play the Sophiſter with ye ; not of their sort who nowadays buzle Young-men's heads with certain empty notions and curious trifles, yet teach them nothing but a more than Womanish obſtinacy of scolding : but I'le imitate those Antients, who, that they might the better avoid that infamous appellation of *Sophi* or *Wise,* chose rather to be call'd Sophiſters. Their business was to celebrate the Praises of the gods and valiant men.

*It was the Goddess of Folly who did the actual lec-
turing, but Erasmus sat behind her and did the
prompting*

And the like Encomium shall ye hear from me, but neither of Hercules nor Solon, but mine own dear Self, that is to say, Folly.

Nor do I esteem those Wise-men a rush, that call it a foolish and insolent thing to praise one's self. Be it as foolish as they would make it, so they confess it proper : and what can be more, than that Folly be her own Trumpet ? For who can set me out better than my self, unless perhaps I could be better known to another than to my self ? Though yet I think it somewhat more modest than the general practice of our Nobles and Wise men, who, throwing away all shame, hire some flattering Orator or Lying Poet, from whose mouth they may hear their praises, that is to say meer lyes ; and yet, composing themselves with a seeming modesty, spread out their Peacock's plumes and erect their Crests, whilst this impudent Flatterer equals a man of nothing to the gods, and proposes him as an absolute pattern of all Virtue that's wholly a stranger to 't, sets out a pittiful Jay in other's Feathers, washes the Blackmoor white, and lastly swells a Gnat to an Elephant.

In short, I will follow that old Proverb that says, "He may lawfully praise himself that lives far from Neighbours." Though, by the way, I cannot but wonder at the ingratitude, shall I say, or negligence of Men, who, notwithstanding they honour me in the first place and are willing enough to confess my bounty, yet not one of them for these so many ages has there been, who in some thankful Oration has set out the praises of Folly; when yet there has not wanted them, whose elaborate endeavours have extol'd Tyrants, Agues, Flyes, Baldness and such other Pests of Nature, to their own loss of both time and sleep.

And now ye shall hear from me a plain extempory speech, but so much the truer. Nor would I have ye think it like the rest of Orators, made for the Ostentation of Wit; for these, as ye know, when they have been beating their heads some thirty years about an Oration, and at last perhaps produce somewhat that was never their own, shall yet swear they compos'd it in three dayes, and that too for diversion: whereas I ever lik't it best to speak whatever came first out.

But let none of ye expect from me, that after the manner of Rhetoricians I should go about to Define what I am, much less use any Division; for I hold it equally unlucky to circumscribe her whose Deity is universal, or make the least Division in that Worship about which every thing is so generally agree'd. Or to what purpose, think ye, should I describe my self, when I am here present before ye, and ye behold me speaking ? For I am, as ye see, that true and onely giver of wealth, whom the Greeks call Μωρία, the Latines *Stultitia,* and our plain English *Folly*.

Or what need was there to have said so much, as if my very looks were not sufficient to inform ye who I am ? Or as if any man, mistaking me for Wisedome, could not at first sight convince himself by my face, the true index of my mind ? I am no Counterfeit, nor do I carry one thing in my looks and another in my breast. No, I am in every respect so like my self, that neither can they dissemble me, who arrogate to themselves the appearance and title of Wisemen, and walk like Asses in Scarlet-hoods; though after all their hypocrisie Midas's ears will discover their Master. A most ingrateful generation of men, that, when they are wholly given up to my Party, are yet publicly asham'd of the name, as taking it for a reproach ; for which cause, since in truth they are Μωρότατοι, Fools, and yet would appear to the World to be Wisemen and Thales's, wee'll ev'n call 'em Μωροσόφους, Wise-fools.

Nor will it be amiss also to imitate the Rhetoricians of our times, who think themselves in a manner Gods, if like Horse-leeches they can but appear to be double-tongu'd ; and believe they have done a mighty act if in their Latin Orations they can but shuffle-in some ends of Greek, like Mosaick-work, though altogether by head and shoulders and less to the purpose. And if they want hard words, they run over some Worm-eaten Manuscript, and pick out half a Dozen of the most old and absolete to confound their Reader, believing, no doubt, that they that understand their meaning will like it the better, and they that do not, will admire it the more by how much the lesse they understand it. Nor is this way of ours of admiring what seems most Forreign without it's particular grace ; for if there happen to be any more ambitious than others, they may give their applause with a smile, and, like the Asse, shake their ears, that they may be thought to understand more than the rest of their neighbours.

Folly's Lineage, Education and Companions

But to come to the purpose : I have giv'n ye my name ; but what Epithet shall I adde ? What but that of the most Foolish ? For by what properer name can so great a goddess as Folly be known to her Disciples ? And because it is not alike known to all from what stock I am sprung, with the Muses' good leave I'le do my endeavour to satisfie you. But yet neither the first Chaos, Orcus, Saturn, or

Japhet, nor any of those thred-bare, musty Gods, were my Father, but Plutus, Riches ; that only he, that is, in spight of Hesiod, Homer, nay and Jupiter himself, *Divum Pater atque Hominum Rex,* the Father of Gods and men ; at whose single beck, as heretofore, so at present, all things Sacred and Prophane are turn'd topsie turvy. According to whose Pleasure War, Peace, Empire, Counsels, Judgements, Assemblies, Wedlocks, Bargains, Leagues, Laws, Arts, all things Light or Serious—I want breath—in short, all the publick and private business of mankind, is govern'd ; without whose help all that Herd of Gods of the Poets' making, and those few of the better sort of the rest, either would not be at all, or if they were, they would be but such as live at home and keep a poor house to themselves. And to whomsoever hee's an Enemy, 'tis not Pallas her self that can befriend him : as on the contrary he whom he favours may lead Jupiter and his Thunder in a string.

This is my father and in him I glory. Nor did he produce me from his brain, as Jupiter that sowre and ill-look'd Pallas ; but of that lovely Nymph call'd Youth, the most beautiful and galliard of all the rest. Nor was I, like that limping Black-smith, begot in the sad and irksome bonds of Matrimony. Yet, mistake me not, 'twas not that blind and decrepit Plutus in Aristophanes that got me, but such as he was in his full ſtrength and pride of youth ; and not that onely, but at such a time when he had been well heated with Nectar, of which he had, at one of the Banquets of the Gods, taken a dose extraordinary.

And as to the place of my birth, forasmuch as nowadays that is look'd upon as a main point of Nobility, it was neither, like Apollo's, in the floating Delos, nor Venus-like on the rolling Sea, nor in any of blind Homer's as blind Caves : but in the fortunate Islands, where all things grew without plowing or sowing ; where neither Labour, nor Old-age, nor Disease, was ever heard of ; and in whose fields neither Daffadil, Mallows, Onyons, Beans, and such contemptible things would ever grow ; but, on the contrary, Rue, Angelica, Buglosse, Marjoram, Trefoiles, Roses, Violets, Lillies, and all the Gardens of Adonis, invite both your sight and your smelling. And being thus born, I did not begin the world, as other Children are wont, with crying; but ſtreight perch'd up and smil'd on my mother. Nor do I envy to the great Jupiter the Goat, his Nurse. forasmuch as I was suckled by two jolly Nymphs, to wit, Drunkenness, the daughter of Bacchus, and Ignorance, of Pan.

And as for such my companions and followers as ye perceive about me, if you have a mind to know who they

The Fortunate Isles

are, ye are not like to be the wiser for me, unlesse it be in Greek: This here, which you observe with that proud cast of her eye, is φιλαυτία, Self-love; She with the smiling countenance, that is ever and anon clapping her hands, is Κολακία, Flattery; She that looks as if she were half asleep, is Λήθη, Oblivion; She that sits leaning on both Elbows with her hands clutch'd together is Μισοπονία, Laziness; She with the Garland on her head, and that smells so strong of perfumes is Ἡδονὴ, Pleasure; She with those staring eyes, moving here and there, is Ἄνοια, Madness; She with the smooth Skin and full pamper'd body is Τρυφὴ, Wantonness; and, as to the two Gods that ye see with them, the one is Κῶμος, Intemperance, the other Νήγρετος ὕπνος, Dead Sleep. These, I say, are my household Servants, and by their faithful Counsels I have subjected all things to my Dominion, and erected an empire over Emperors themselves. Thus have ye had my Lineage, Education, and Companions.

Whoever Intends to have Children must have Recourse to Folly

And now, lest I may seem to have taken upon me the name of Goddess without cause, you shall in the next place understand how far my Deity extends, and what

advantage by 't I have brought both to Gods and Men.
For, if it was not unwisely said by some body, that this
only is to be a God, To help Men ; and if they are de-
servedly enroll'd among the Gods that firſt brought in
Corn and Wine and such other things as are for the common good of mankind, why am not I of right the ἄλφα,
or firſt, of all the gods ? who being but one, yet beſtow
all things on all men. For firſt, What is more sweet or
more precious than Life ? And yet from whom can it
more properly be said to come than from me ? For neither
the Crab-favour'd Pallas's spear, nor the Cloud-gathering
Jupiter's Shield, either beget, or propagate mankind ; But
even he himself, the Father of Gods, and King of Men
at whose very beck the Heavens shake, muſt lay-by his
forked thunder, and those looks wherewith he conquer'd
the Gyants, and with which at pleasure he frights the reſt
of the Gods, and like a Common Stage-player put on a
Disguise, as often as he goes about that, which now and
then he do's, that is to say the getting of children : and
the Stoicks too, that conceive themselves next to the Gods,
yet shew me one of them, nay the veryeſt Bygot of the
Sect, and if he do not put off his beard, the badge of Wisdom, though yet it be no more than what is common
with him and Goats ; yet at leaſt he muſt lay-by his super-

cilious Gravity, smooth his forehead, shake off his rigid
Principles, and for some time commit an act of folly and
dotage. In fine, that Wiseman who ever he be, if he intends
to have Children muſt have recourse to me.

But tell me, I beseech ye, What Man is that would sub-
mit his neck to the Noose of Wedlock, if as Wisemen
should, he did but firſt truly weigh the inconvenience of
the thing ? Or what Woman is there would ever go to
't did she seriously consider either the peril of Child-bear-
ing, or the trouble of bringing them up ? So then, if ye
owe your beings to Wedlock, ye owe that Wedlock to
this my follower, Madness ; and what ye owe to me I
have already told ye.

Again, she that has but once try'd what it is, would she,
do ye think, make a second venture, if it were not for my
other Companion, Oblivion ? Nay, even Venus her self,
notwithſtanding what ever Lucretius has said, would not
deny but that all her vertue were lame and fruitless without the help of my Deity. For out of that little, odd, ridiculous May-game came the supercilious Philosophers, in
whose room have succeeded a kind of people the world
calls Monks, Cardinals, Prieſts, and the moſt holy Popes.
And Laſtly, all that Rabble of the Poets'-Gods, with which
Heaven is so thwack't and throng'd, that though it be of

so vaſt an extent, they are hardly able to croud one by another.

But I think it a small matter that ye thus owe your beginning of life to me, unless I also shew you that whatever benefit you receive in the progress of it is of my gift likewise. For what other is this ? Can that be call'd life where ye take away pleasure ? Oh ! Do ye like what I say ? I knew none of you could have so little Wit, or so much folly, or Wisdom rather, as to be of any other opinion. For even the Stoicks themselves, that so severely cry'd down pleasure, did but handsomly dissemble, and rail'd againſt it to the common People, to no other end but that having discourag'd them from it, they might the more plentifully enjoy it themselves.

Folly Seasons Man's Life With Pleasure

But tell me, by Jupiter, what part of man's life is that that is not sad, crabbed, unpleasant, insipid, troublesome, unless it be seasoned with Pleasure, that is to say, Folly ? For the proof of which the never-sufficiently prais'd Sophocles, in that his happy Elogy of us "To know nothing is the onely happiness", might be Authority enough, but that I intend to take every particular by it's self.

And firſt, Who knows not but a man's Infancy is the

merriest part of life to himself, and most acceptable to others ? For what is that in them which we kiss, embrace, cherish, nay Enemies succour, but this witchcraft of Folly, which wise Nature did of purpose give them into the world with them, that they might the more pleasantly passe-over the toil of Education, and as it were flatter the care and diligence of their Nurses.

And then for Youth, which is in such reputation everywhere, how do all men favour it, study to advance it and lend it their helping hand ? And whence, I pray, all this Grace ? Whence but from me ? by whose kindness, as it understands as little as may be, it is also for that reason the higher privileged from exceptions ; and I am mistaken if, when it is grown up and by experience and discipline brought to savour something like Man, if in the same instant that beauty does not fade, it's liveliness decay, it's pleasantness grow flat, and it's briskness fail.

And by how much the further it runs from me, by so much the less it lives, till it comes to the burthen of Old age, not onely hateful to others, but to it self also. Which also were altogether insupportable did not I pitty it's condition, in being present with it, and, as the Poets'-gods were wont to assist such as were dying with some pleasant Metamorphosis, help their decrepitness as much as in me lies by bringing them back to a second childhood, from whence they are not improperly called Twice-Children. Which, if ye ask me how I do it, I shall not be shy in the point. I bring them to our River Lethe (for it's spring-head rises in the Fortunate Islands, and that other of Hell is but a Brook in comparison), from which, as soon as they have drunk down a long forgetfulness, they wash away by degrees the perplexity of their minds, and so wax young again.

But perhaps you'll say, They are foolish and doting. Admit it ; 'tis the very essence of Child-hood ; as if to be such were not to be a fool, or that that condition had any thing pleasant in it, but that it understood nothing. For who would not look upon that Child as a Prodigy that should have as much Wisdome as a Man ?—according to that common Proverb, "I do not like a Child that is a Man too soon." Or who would endure a Converse or Friendship with that Old-man, who to so large an experi-ence of things, had joyn'd an equal strength of mind and sharpness of judgement ? And therefore for this reason it is that Old-age dotes ; and that it does so, it is beholding to me. Yet, not withstanding, is this dotard exempt from all those cares that distract a Wise man ; he is not the less pot-Companion, nor is he sensible of that burden of life,

which the more manly Age finds enough to do to ſtand
upright under 't. And sometimes too, like Plautus's Old-
man, he returns to his three Letters, A.M.O., the moſt
unhappy of all things living, if he rightly underſtood
what he did in 't. And yet, so much do I befriend him,
that I make him well receiv'd of his friends, and no unpleasant Companion ; for as much as, according to Homer,
Neſtor's discourse was pleasanter than Honey, whereas
Achilles's was both bitter and malicious ; and that of Old-
men, as he has it in another place, florid. In which respeсt,
also, they have this advantage of children, in that they
want the onely pleasure of t' others life, we'll suppose it
pratling.

Adde to this that old men are more eagerly delighted
with children, and they, again, with Old-men. "Like to
like", quoth the Divel to the Collier. For what difference
between them, but that the one has more wrinckles and
years upon his head than the other ? Otherwise, the bright-
ness of their hair, toothless mouth, weakness of body, love
of Milk, broken speech, chatting, toying, forgetfulness,
inadvertency, and briefly, all other their aсtions, agree in
every thing. And by how much the nearer they approach
to this Old-age, by so much they grow backward into the
likeness of Children, until like them they pass from life

to death, without any weariness of the one, or sense of t' other.

And now, let him that will compare the benefits they receive by me, with the Metamorphoses of the Gods ; of whom, I ſhall not mention what they have done in their pettiſh humours, but where they have been moſt favourable : turning one into a Tree, another into a Bird, a third into a Graſhopper, Serpent, or the like. As if there were any difference between periſhing, and being another thing ! But I reſtore the same man to the beſt and happieſt part of his life. And if Men would but refrain from all commerce with Wisdom, and give up themselves to be govern'd by me, they should never know what it were to be old, but solace themselves with a perpetual youth.

Do but observe our grim Philosophers that are perpetually beating their brains on knotty Subjeſts, and for the moſt part you'll find 'em grown old before they are scarce young. And whence is it, but that their continual and reſtless thoughts insensibly prey upon their spirits, and dry up their Radical Moiſture ? Whereas, on the contrary, my fat fools are as plump and round as a Weſtphalian Hogg, and never sensible of old age, unless perhaps, as sometimes it rarely happens, they come to be infeſted with Wisdom ; so hard a thing it is for a man

*On the other hand my fat fools are as plump and
round as Westphalian hogs*

to be happy in all things. And to this purpose is that no small testimony of the Proverb, that says, " Folly is the onely thing that keeps Youth at a stay, and Old age afar off ; " as it is verifi'd in the Brabanders, of whom there goes this common saying, " That Age, which is wont to render other Men wiser, makes them the greater Fools." And yet there is scarce any Nation of a more jocund converse, or that is less sensible of the misery of Old age, than they are. And to these, as in scituation, so for manner of living, come nearest my friends the Hollanders. And why should I not call them mine, since they are so diligent observers of me that they are commonly call'd by my name ?—of which they are so far from being asham'd, they rather pride themselves in 't.

Let the foolish world then be packing and seek out Medeas, Circes, Venuses, Auroras and I know not what other Fountains of restoring Youth. I am sure I am the onely person that both can, and have made it good. 'Tis I alone that have that wonderful Juice with which Memnon's daughter prolong'd the youth of her Grandfather Tithon. I am that Venus by whose favour Phaon became so young again that Sappho fell in love with him. Mine are those Herbs, if yet there be any such, mine those Charms, and mine that Fountain, that not only restores departed Youth but, which is more desirable, preserves it perpetual. And if ye all subscribe to this Opinion, that nothing is better than Youth, or more execrable than Age, I conceive you cannot but see how much ye are indebted to me, that have retain'd so great a good, and shut out so great an evil.

The Gods Play the Fool

But why do I altogether spend my breath in speaking of Mortals ? View Heaven round, and let him that will, reproach me with my name, if he find any one of the Gods that were not ſtinking and contemptible, were he not made acceptable by my Deity. Whence is it that Bacchus is always a Stripling, and bushy-hair'd ? but because he is mad, and drunk, and spends his life in Drinking, Dancing, Revels, and May-games, not having so much as the leaſt society with Pallas. And laſtly, he is so far from desiring to be accounted wise, that he delights to be worshipp'd with Sports and Gambals ; nor is he displeas'd with the Proverb that gave him the sirname of Fool, " A greater Fool than Bacchus "; which name of his was chang'd to Morychus, for that sitting before the gates of his Temple, the wanton Countrey people were wont to bedaub him with new Wine and

Figgs. And of scoffs, what not, hath not the antient Come-
dies thrown on him ? O foolish God, say they, and worthy
to be born as thou wert of thy Father's thigh ! And yet,
who had not rather be thy Fool and Sot, alwayes merry,
ever young, and making sport for other people, than
either Homer's Jupiter, with his crooked Councels, terrible to every one ; or old Pan with his Hubbubs ; or
smutty Vulcan half-cover'd with Cinders ; or even Pallas
her self, so dreadful with her Gorgon's Head and Spear
and a Countenance like Bull-beef ?

Why is Cupid always Pourtrai'd like a Boy, but because he is a very Wagg, and can neither do nor so much
as think of any thing sober ? Why Venus ever in her
prime, but because of her affinity with me ? Witness that
colour of her Hair, so resembling my Father, from whence
she is call'd the golden Venus ; and lastly, ever laughing,
if ye give any credit to the Poets, or their followers the
Statuaries. What Deity did the Romans ever more religiously adore than that of Flora, the foundress of all
pleasure ?

Nay, if ye should but diligently search the lives of the
most sowre and morose of the Gods out of Homer and
the rest of the Poets, you would find 'em all but so many
pieces of Folly. And to what purpose should I run over

any of the other gods' tricks when ye know enough of Jupiter's loose Loves ? when that chaſt Diana shall so far forget her Sexe as to be ever hunting and ready to perish for Endymion ? But I had rather they should hear these things from Momus, from whom heretofore they were wont to have their shares, till in one of their angry humours they tumbled him, together with Ate, Goddess of Mischief, down headlong to the Earth, because his wisdom, forsooth, unseasonably disturb'd their happiness. Nor since that dares any mortal give him harbour, though I muſt confess there wanted little but that he had been receiv'd into the Courts of Princes, had not my companion Flattery reign'd in chief there, with whom and t' other there is no more correspondence than between Lambs and Wolves.

From whence it is that the Gods play the fool with the greater liberty and more content to themselves, " doing all things carelessly," as says Father Homer, that is to say, without any one to correct them. For what ridiculous ſtuff is there which that ſtump of the Fig-tree Priapus does not afford 'em ? what Tricks and Legerdemains with which Mercury does not cloak his thefts ? what buffonry that Vulcan is not guilty of, while one while with his poltfoot, another with his smutcht muzzle, an-

other with his impertinencies, he makes sport for the rest
of the Gods ? As also that old Silenus with his Countrey-
dances, Polyphemus footing time to his Cyclops hammers,
the Nymphs with their Jiggs, and Satyrs with their An-
ticks ; whilst Pan makes 'em all twitter with some coarse
Ballad, which yet they had rather hear than the Muses
themselves, and chiefly when they are well whitled with
Nectar. Besides, what should I mention what these Gods
do when they are half drunk ? Now by my troth, so foolish that I my self can hardly refrain laughter. But in these
matters 'twere better we remember'd Harpocrates, lest
some Eves-dropping God or other take us whispering
that which Momus onely has the priviledge of speaking at
length.

Look Down a Little on the Earth

And therefore, according to Homer's example I think
it high time to leave the Gods to themselves, and look
down a little on the Earth ; wherein likewise you'll find
nothing frolick or fortunate, that it ows not to me. So
provident has that great Parent of Mankind, Nature, been,
that there should not be any thing without it's mixture,
and as it were seasoning of Folly. For since according to
the definition of the Stoicks, Wisdom is nothing else than

to be govern'd by reason; and on the contrary Folly, to be giv'n up to the will of our Passions; that the life of man might not be altogether disconsolate and hard to away with, of how much more Passion than Reason has Jupiter compos'd us? putting in, as one would say, "scarce half an ounce to a pound". Besides, he has confin'd Reason to a narrow corner of the brain, and left all the rest of the body to our Passions; as also set up, against this one, two as it were, masterless Tyrants—Anger, that possesseth the region of the heart, and consequently the very Fountain of life, the Heart it self; and Lust, that stretcheth its Empire every where. Against which double force how powerful Reason is, let common experience declare, inasmuch as she, which yet is all she can do, may call out to us till she be hoarse again, and tell us the Rules of Honesty and Vertue; while they give up the Reins to their Governour, and make a hideous clamour, till at last being wearied, he suffer himself to be carried whither they please to hurry him.

But forasmuch as such as are born to the business of the world have some little sprinklings of Reason more than the rest, yet that they may the better manage it, even in this as well as in other things, they call me to counsel;

and I give 'em such as is worthy of my self, to wit That
they take to 'em a wife—a silly thing, God wot, and foolish, yet wanton and pleasant, by which means the rough-
ness of the Masculine temper is season'd and sweeten'd
by her folly. For in that Plato seems to doubt under which
Genus he should put woman, to wit that of rational Creatures or Brutes, he intended no other in it than to shew
the apparent folly of the Sexe. For if perhaps any of them
goes about to be thought wiser than the reſt, what else
does she do but play the fool twice, as if a man should
" teach a Cow to dance ", " a thing quite againſt the hair ".
For as it doubles the crime if any one should put a disguise
upon Nature, or endeavour to bring her to that she will
in no wise bear, according to that Proverb of the Greeks,
" An Ape is an Ape, though clad in Scarlet "; so a woman
is a woman ſtill, that is to say foolish, let her put on what
ever Vizard she please.

But, by the way, I hope that Sexe is not so foolish as
to take offence at this, that I my self, being a woman, and
Folly too, have attributed Folly to them. For if they weigh
it right, they needs muſt acknowledg that they owe it to
Folly that they are more fortunate than men. As firſt their
Beauty, which, and that not without cause, they prefer

before every thing, since by its means they exercise a Tyranny even upon Tyrants themselves; otherwise, whence proceeds that sowre look, rough skin, bushy beard and such other things as speak plain Old age in a man, but from that Disease of Wisdom ? whereas women's Cheeks are ever plump and smooth, their Voice small, their Skin soft, as if they imitated a certain kind of perpetual Youth.

Again, what greater thing do they wish in their whole lives, than that they may please the Men ? For to what other purpose are all those Dresses, Washes, Baths, Curlings, Slops, Perfumes, and those several little tricks of setting their Faces, painting their Eye-brows, and smoothing their Skins ? And now tell me, what higher Letters of Recommendation have they to men than this Folly ? For what is it they do not permit 'em to do ? and to what other purpose than that of pleasure ? wherein yet their folly is not the least thing that pleaseth ; which how true it is, I think no one will deny, that does but consider with himself, what foolish Discourse and odd Gambals pass between a man and his woman, as oft as he has a mind to be gamesome ? And so I have shown ye whence the first and chiefest delight of man's life springs.

Folly Makes Society Delightful

But there are some, you'll say, and those too none of
the youngeſt, that have a greater kindness for the Pot than
the Petticoat, and place their chiefeſt pleasure in good
fellowship. If there can be any great entertainment without a woman at it, let others look to 't. This I am sure,
there was never any pleasant which Folly gave not the
relish to. Insomuch that if they find no occasion of Laughter, they send for " one that may make it ", or hire some
Buffon flatterer, whose ridiculous discourse may put by
the Gravity of the company. For to what purpose were it
to clogg our Stomacks with Dainties, Junkets and the
like Stuff, unless our Eyes and Ears, nay whole Mind,
were likewise entertain'd with Jeſts, Merriments and
Laughter ? But of these kind of second Courses I am the
onely Cook ; though yet those ordinary practises of our
Feaſts, as choosing a King, throwing Dice, drinking
Healths, trouling it Round, dancing the Cushion and the
like, were not invented by the seven Wise Men but my
Self, and that too for the common pleasure of Mankind.
The nature of all which things is such, that the more of
Folly they have, the more they conduce to Humane Life,
which, if it were unpleasant, did not deserve the same of

Life ; and other than such it could not well be, did not these kind of Diversions wype away tediousnesse, nexte cosyn to the other.

But perhaps there are some that neglect this way of pleasure, and reſt satisfi'd in the enjoyment of their Friends, calling friendship the moſt desirable of all things ; more necessary than either air, fire, or water ; so delectable, that he that shall take it out of the World had as good put out the Sun ; and laſtly so commendable, if yet that make any thing to the matter, that neither the Philosophers themselves doubted to reckon it among their chiefeſt good. But what if I shew you that I am both the beginning and end of this so great good also ? Nor shall I go about to prove it by Fallacies, Sorites, Dilemmas, or other the like subtilties of Logicians, but after my blunt way, point out the thing as clearly as 'twere with my finger.

And now tell me, if to wink, slip over, be blind at, or deceiv'd in, the vices of our friends, nay, to admire and esteem them for Virtues, be not at leaſt the next degree to folly ? What is it when one kisses his Miſtresses freckle Neck, another the Wart on her Nose ? When a Father shall swear his squint-ey'd Child is more lovely than Venus ? What is this, I say, but meer folly ? And so, per-haps you'l cry, it is ; and yet 'tis this onely that joyns

What father does not swear his squint-eyed child to
be lovelier than Venus herself?

friends together, and continues them so joyn'd. I speak
of ordinary men, of whom none are born without their
imperfections, and happy is he that is prest with the
least : for among wise Princes there is either no friendship at all, or if there be, 'tis unpleasant and reserv'd, and
that too but amongst a very few, 'twere a crime to say
none. For that the greatest part of mankind are fools,
nay there is not any one that dotes not in many things ;
and friendship, you know, is seldome made but amongst
equalls. And yet if it should so happen that there were
a mutual good-will between them, it is in no wise firm
nor very long liv'd ; that is to say, among such as are
morose and more circumspect than needs, as being Eagle-
sighted into his friends' faults, but so blear-ey'd to their
own that they take not the least notice of the Wallet that
hangs behind their own Shoulders.

Since then the nature of Man is such that there is scarce
any one to be found that is not subject to many errors,
add to this the great diversity of minds and studies, so
many slips, oversights and chances of humane life, and
how is it possible there should be any true friendship between those Argus's, so much as one hour, were it not
for that which the Greeks excellently call εὐήθειαν ? and
you may render by Folly or good Nature, chuse you

whether. But what ? Is not the Author and Parent of all
our Love, Cupid, as blind as a beetle ? and as with him
all colours agree, so from him is it that every one likes
his own Sweeter-kin beſt, though never so ugly, and " that
an old man dotes on his old wife, and a boy on his girle ".
These things are not onely done every where but laught at
too, yet as ridiculous as they are, they make society pleasant, and, as it were, glew it together.

And what has been said of Friendship may more reasonably be presum'd of Matrimony, which in truth is no
other than an inseparable conjunction of life. Good God !
What Divorces, or what not worse than that, would daily
happen, were not the converse between a man and his
wife supported and cherished by flattery, apishnesse, gen-
tlenesse, ignorance, dissembling, certain Retainers of mine
also ! Whoop holiday ! how few marriages should we
have, if the Husband should but through-examin how
many tricks his pretty little Mop of Modeſty has plaid
before she was marry'd ! And how fewer of them would
hold together, did not most of the Wife's actions escape
the Husband's knowledge through his neglect or sottish-
ness ! And for this also ye are beholding to me, by whose
means it is that the Husband is pleasant to his Wife, the
Wife to her Husband, and the house kept in quiet. A man

is laught at, when seeing his Wife weeping he licks up
her tears. But how much happier is it to be thus deceiv'd
than by being troubled with jealousie, not onely to tor-
ment himself, but set all things in a hubbub !

In fine, I am so necessary to the making of all society
and manner of life both delightful and lasting, that neither
would the people long endure their Governors, nor the
Servant his Master, nor the Master his Footman, nor the
Scholar his Tutor, nor one friend another, nor the Wife
her Husband, nor the Userer the Borrower, nor a Souldier
his Commander, nor one Companion another, unlesse all
of them had their interchangeable failings, one while
flattering, other while prudently conniving, and generally
sweetning one another with some small relish of Folly.

It Is Necessary that Every one Flatter Himself

And now you'd think I had said all, but ye shall hear yet
greater things. Will he, I pray, love any one that hates
himself ? Or ever agree with another who is not at peace
with himself ? Or beget pleasure in another that is troublesome to himself ? I think no one will say it that is not
more foolish than Folly. And yet, if ye should exclude
me, there 's no man but would be so far from enduring

another that he would ſtink in his own noſtrils, be nause-
ated with his own actions, and himself become odious
to himself; forasmuch as Nature, in too many things
rather a Stepdame than a Parent to us, has imprinted that
evil in men, especially such as have leaſt judgment, that
every one repents him of his own condition and admires
that of others. Whence it comes to pass that all her gifts,
elegancy and graces corrupt and perish.

For what benefit is Beauty, the greateſt blessing of
Heaven, if it be mixt with affectation? What Youth, if
corrupted with the severity of old Age? Laſtly, what is
that in the whole business of a man's life he can do with
any grace to himself or others—for it is not so much a
thing of Art, as the very life of every Action, that it be
done with a good meen—unlesse this my friend and companion, Self-love, be present with it?

Nor does she without cause supply me the place of
a Siſter, since her whole endeavours are to act my part
every where. For what is more foolish than for a man
to ſtudy nothing else than how to please himself? To
make himself the object of his own admiration? And
yet, what is there that is either delightful or taking, nay
rather what not the contrary, that a man does againſt
the hair? Take away this Salt of life, and the Orator

may ev'n sit still with his Action, the Musitian with all his division will be able to please no man, the Player be hist off the Stage, the Poet and all his Muses ridiculous, the Painter with his Art contemptible, and the Physitian with all his Slip-slops go a begging. Lastly, thou wilt be taken for an Ugly fellow instead of a Beautiful, for Old and Decrepit instead of Youthful, and a Beast instead of a Wise man, a Child instead of Eloquent, and instead of a well-bred man, a clown. So necessary a thing it is that every one flatter himself, and commend himself to himself before he can be commended by others.

Lastly, since it is the chiefest point of happinesse "that a man is willing to be what he is", you have further abridg'd in this my Self-love, that no man's asham'd of his own face, no man of his own wit, no man of his own parentage, no man of his own house, no man of his manner of living, nor any man of his own Country; so that a Highlander has no desire to change with an Italian, a Thracian with an Athenian, nor a Scythian for the fortunate Islands. O the singular care of Nature, that in so great a variety of things has made all equal! Where she has been sometime sparing of her gifts she has recompenc'd it with the more of self-Love; though here, I must confess, I speak foolishly, it being the greatest of all other

her Gifts : to say nothing that no great action was ever attempted without my Motion, or Art brought to perfection without my help.

A Wise Man Should Abstain from Public Business

Is not War the very Root and Matter of all Fam'd Enterprises ? And yet what more foolish than to undertake it for I know not what trifles, especially when both Parties are sure to lose more than they get by the bargain ? For of those that are slain, not a word of them ; and for the rest, when both sides are close engag'd " and the Trumpets make an ugly noise ", what use of those Wise men, I pray, that are so exhaust with study that their thin cold Blood has scarce any spirits left ? No, it must be those blunt fat fellows, that by how much the more they exceed in Courage, fall short in Understanding. Unless perhaps one had rather chuse Demosthenes for a Souldier, who, following the example of Archilochius, threw away his Arms and betook him to his Heels e're he had scarce seen his Enemy ; as ill a Souldier, as happy an Orator.

But Counsel, you'll say, is not of least concern in matters of War. In a General I grant it ; but this thing of Warring is no part of Philosophy, but manag'd by Parasites, Pan-

The glories of the triumphant warrior

dars, Thieves, Cut-throats, Plow-men, Sots, Spendthrifts
and such other Dregs of Mankind, not Philosophers ; who
how unapt they are even for common converse, let Socrates,
whom the Oracle of Apollo, though not so wisely, judg'd
" the wiseſt of all men living ", be witness ; who ſtepping
up to speak somewhat, I know not what, in publique, was
forc'd to come down again well laught at for his pains.
Though yet in this he was not altogether a fool, that he
refus'd the appellation of Wise, and returning it back to
the Oracle, deliver'd his opinion That a wise man should
abſtain from medling with publique business ; unless
perhaps he should have rather admonisht us to beware of
Wisdom if we intended to be reckon'd among the number
of men, there being nothing but his Wisdom that firſt
accus'd and afterwards sentenc't him to the drinking of his
poison'd Cup. For while, as ye find him in Ariſtophanes,
Philosophying about Clouds and Ideas, measuring how
far a Flea could leap, and admiring that so small a creature as a Flye should make so great a buzze, he medled
not with any thing that concern'd common life. But his
Maſter being in danger of his head, his Scholar Plato is
at hand, to wit that famous Patron, that being diſturb'd
with the noise of the people, could not go through half
his firſt Sentence.

What should I speak of Theophrastus, who being about to make an Oration, became as dumb as if he had met a Wolfe in his way, which yet would have put courage in a Man of War ? Or Isocrates, that was so cowhearted that he durst never attempt it ? Or Tully, that great Founder of the Roman Eloquence, that could never begin to speak without an odd kind of trembling, like a Boy that had got the Hick-cop ; which Fabius interprets as an argument of a wise Oratour and one that was sensible of what he was doing ; and while he sayes it, does he not plainly confess that Wisdom is a great obstacle to the true management of business ? What would become of 'em, think ye, were they to fight it out at blows, that are so dead through fear, when the Contest is only with empty words ?

And next to these is cry'd up, forsooth, that goodly sentence of Plato's : " Happy is that Commonwealth where a Philosopher is Prince, or whose Prince is addicted to Philosophy ". When yet if ye consult Historians, you'll find no Princes more pestilent to the Commonwealth than where the Empire has fall'n to some smatterer in Philosophy or one given to Letters. To the truth of which I think the Catoes give sufficient credit ; of whom the one was ever disturbing the peace of the Commonwealth with his hair-brain'd accusations ; the other, while he too wisely vindicated its liberty, quite overthrew it. Add to this the Bruti, Cassii, nay Cicero himself, that was no less pernicious to the Commonwealth of Rome than was Demosthenes to that of Athens. Besides M. Antoninus (that I may give ye one instance that there was once one good Emperour ; for with much ado I can make it out) was become burthensome and hated of his Subjects, upon no other score but that he was so great a Philosopher. But admitting him good, he did the Commonwealth more hurt in leaving behind him such a Son as he did, than ever he did it good by his own Government.

For these kind of Men that are so given up to the study of Wisdome are generally most unfortunate, but chiefly in their Children ; Nature, it seems, so providently ordering it, lest this mischief of Wisdome should spread farther among mankind. For which reason 'tis manifest why Cicero's Son was so degenerate, and that wise Socrates's Children, as one has well observ'd, were more like their Mother than their Father, that is to say, Fools.

However this were to be born with, if only as to publick Employments they were "Like a Sow upon a pair of organs", were they any thing apter to discharge even the common Offices of Life. Invite a Wise man to a Feast and he'll spoil the company, either with Morose silence or troublesome Disputes. Take him out to Dance, and you'l swear "a Cow would have don 't better". Bring him to the Theatre, and his very looks are enough to spoil all, till like Cato he take an occasion of withdrawing rather than put off his supercilious gravity. Let him fall into discourse, and he shall make more sudden stops than if he had a Woolf before him. Let him buy, or sell, or in short go about any of those things without which there is no living in this world, and you'l say this piece of Wisdom were rather a Stock than a Man, of so little use is he to himself, Country, or Friends ; and all because he is wholly ignorant of common things, and lives a course of life quite different from the people ; by which means 'tis impossible but that he contract a popular odium, to wit, by reason of the great diversity of their life and souls. For what is there at all done among men that is not full of Folly, and that too from fools and to fools ? Against which universal practice if any single one shall dare to set up his throat, my advice to him is, that following the example of Timon, he retire into some desart and there enjoy his wisdome to himself.

Invite a wise man to a feast and he will spoil the company with either morose silence or troublesome disputes

What is Life but a kind of Comedy?

But, to return to my design, what power was it that drew those ſtony, oken and wild people into Cities, but flattery ? For nothing else is signify'd by Amphion and Orpheus's Harp. What was it that, when the common people of Rome were like to have destroy'd all by their Mutiny, reduc'd them to Obedience ? Was it a Philosophical Oration ? Least. But a ridiculous and childish Fable, of the Belly and the rest of the Members. And as good success had Themiſtocles in his of the Fox and Hedghog. What wise man's Oration could ever have done so much with the people as Sertorius's invention of his white Hind ? Or his ridiculous Emblem of pulling off a Horse's Tail hair by hair ? Or as Lycurgus's his example of his two Whelps ? To say nothing of Minos and Numa, both which rul'd their foolish multitudes with Fabulous Inventions ; with which kind of Toyes that great and powerful beaſt, the People, are led any way.

Again what City ever receiv'd Plato's or Ariſtotle's Laws, or Socrates's Precepts ? But, on the contrary, what made the Decii devote themselves to the Infernal Gods, or Q. Curtius to leap into the Gulph, but an empty vain glory, a moſt bewitching Sirene ? And yet 'tis ſtrange it

should be so condemn'd by those wise Philosophers. For
what is more foolish, say they, than for a Suppliant Suiter
to flatter the people, to buy their favour with gifts, to
court the applauses of so many fools, to please himself
with their Acclamations, to be carri'd on the people's
shoulders as in triumph, and have a brazen Statue in the
Market place ? Add to this the adoption of Names and
Sirnames ; those Divine Honours given to a man of no
Reputation, and the Deification of the moſt wicked Tyrants with publique Ceremonies ; moſt foolish things,
and such as one Democritus is too little to laugh at. Who
denies it ? And yet from this root sprang all the great
Acts of the Heroes, which the Pens of so many Eloquent
men have extoll'd to the Skies. In a word, this Folly is
that that lai'd the foundation of Cities ; and by it, Empire,
Authority, Religion, Policy and publique Actions are preserv'd ; neither is there any thing in Humane Life that
is not a kind of paſtime of Folly.

But to speak of Arts, what set men's wits on work to
invent and transmit to Poſterity so many Famous, as they
conceive, pieces of Learning, but the thirſt of Glory ?
With so much loss of sleep, such pains and travel, have
the moſt foolish of men thought to purchase themselves
a kind of I know not what Fame, than which nothing

But to speak of the arts—with so much loss of sleep,
such pain and travail have the most foolish of men
thought to purchase themselves fame

can be more vain. And yet notwithstanding, ye owe this advantage to Folly, and which is the most delectable of all other, that ye reap the benefit of other men's madness.

And now, having vindicated to my self the praise of Fortitude and Industry, what think ye if I do the same by that of Prudence ? But some will say, You may as well joyn Fire and Water. It may be so. But yet I doubt not but to succeed even in this also, if, as ye have done hitherto, ye will but favour me with your attention. And first, if Prudence depends upon Experience, to whom is the honour of that name more proper ? To the Wiseman, who partly out of modesty and partly distrust of himself, attempts nothing ; or the Fool, whom neither Modesty which he never had, nor Danger which he never considers, can discourage from any thing ? The Wiseman has recourse to the Books of the Antients, and from thence picks nothing but subtilties of words. The Fool, in undertaking and venturing on the business of the world, gathers, if I mistake not, the true Prudence, such as Homer though blind may be said to have seen, when he said " The burnt child dreads the fire ". For there are two main obstacles to the knowledge of things, Modesty that casts a mist before the understanding, and Fear that, having fanci'd a danger, disswades us from the attempt. But from these

Folly sufficiently frees us, and few there are that rightly understand of what great advantage it is to blush at nothing and attempt every thing.

But if ye had rather take Prudence for that that consists in the judgment of things, hear me, I beseech ye, how far they are from it that yet crack of the name. For first 'tis evident that all Humane things, like Alcibiades's Sileni or rural Gods, carry a double face, but not the least alike ; so that what at first sight seems to be death, if you view it narrowly may prove to be life ; and so the contrary. What appears beautiful may chance to be deform'd ; what wealthy, a very begger ; what infamous, praiseworthy ; what learned, a dunce ; what lusty, feeble ; what jocund, sad ; what noble, base ; what lucky, unfortunate ; what friendly, an enemy ; and what healthful, noisome. In short, view the inside of these Sileni, and you'll find them quite other than what they appear ; which, if perhaps it shall not seem so Philosophically spoken, I'll make it plain to you " after my blunt way ". Who would not conceive a Prince a great Lord and abundant in every thing ? But yet being so ill furnisht with the gifts of the mind, and ever thinking he shall never have enough, he's the poorest of all men. And then for his mind so giv'n up to Vice, 'tis a shame how it inslaves him. I might in like manner Philosophy of the rest ; but let this one, for example's sake, be enough.

Yet why this ? will some one say. Have patience, and I'll shew ye what I drive at. If any one seeing a Player acting his Part on a Stage, should go about to strip him of his disguise, and shew him to the people in his true Native Form, would he not, think ye, not onely spoil the whole design of the Play, but deserve himself to be pelted off with stones as a Phantastical Fool, and one out of his wits ? But nothing is more common with them than such changes ; the same person one while personating a Woman, and another while a Man ; now a Youngster, and by and by a grim Seigniour ; now a King , and presently a Peasant ; now a God, and in a trice agen an ordinary Fellow. But to discover this were to spoil all, it being the onely thing that entertains the Eyes of the Spectators.

And what is all this Life but a kind of Comedy, wherein men walk up and down in one another's Disguises, and Act their respective Parts, till the property-man brings 'em back to the Tyring House. And yet he often orders a different Dress, and makes him that came but just now off in the Robes of a King, put on the Raggs of a Begger. Thus are all things represented by Counterfeit, and yet without this there were no living.

And here if any wise man, as it were dropt from Heaven, should ſtart up and cry, This great thing, whom the World looks upon for a God and I know not what, is not so much as a Man, for that like a Beaſt he is led by his Passions, but the worſt of Slaves, inasmuch as he gives himself up willingly to so many and such deteſtable Maſters. Again if he should bid a man that were bewailing the death of his Father to laugh, for that he now began to live by having got an Eſtate, without which Life is but a kind of Death ; or call another that were boaſting of his Family, ill begotten or base, because he is so far remov'd from Vertue that is the only Fountain of Nobility ; and so of the reſt : what else would he get by 't but be thought himself Mad and Frantick ? For as nothing is more foolish than prepoſterous Wisdome, so nothing is more unadvised than a froward unseasonable Prudence. And such is his that does not comply with the present time " and order himself as the Market goes ", but forgetting that Law of Feaſts, " either drink or begon ", undertakes to disprove a common receiv'd Opinion. Whereas on the contrary 'tis the part of a truly Prudent man not to be wise beyond his Condition, but either to take no notice of what the world does, or run with it for company. But this is foolish, you'll say ; nor shall I deny it, provided always ye be so

civil on t' other side as to confess that this is to Act a Part
in that World.

If All Men Were Wise

But, O ye Gods, " shall I speak or hold my tongue ? "
But why should I be silent in a thing that is more true
than truth it self ? However it might not be amiss perhaps
in so great an Affair, to call forth the Muses from Helicon,
since the Poets so often invoke 'em upon every foolish
occasion. Be present then awhile, and assist me, ye Daughters of Jupiter, while I make it out that there is no way to
that so much Fam'd Wisdome, nor access to that Fortress
as they call it of Happiness, but under the Banner of Folly.
And first 'tis agreed of all hands that our passions belong
to Folly ; inasmuch as we judge a wise Man from a Fool
by this, that the one is order'd by them, the other by
Reason ; and therefore the Stoicks remove from a wise
man all disturbances of Mind as so many Diseases. But
these Passions do not onely the Office of a Tutor to such
as are making towards the Port of Wisdom, but are in
every exercise of Vertue as it were Spurs and Incentives,
nay and Encouragers to well doing : which though that
great Stoick Seneca most strongly denys, and takes from
a wise man all affections whatever, yet in doing that he

leaves him not so much as a Man, but rather a new kind of God, that was never yet, nor ever like to be. Nay, to speak plainer, he sets up a ſtony Semblance of a Man, void of all Sense and common feeling of Humanity. And much good to them with this Wise Man of theirs ; let them enjoy him to themselves, love him without Competitors, and live with him in Plato's Common-wealth, the Countrey of Ideas, or Tantalus's Orchards.

For who would not shun and ſtartle at such a man, as at some unnatural accident or Spirit ? A man dead to all sense of Nature and common affeҁions, and no more mov'd with Love or Pity than if he were a Flint or Rock ; whose censure nothing escapes ; that commits no errors himself, but has a Lynx's eyes upon others ; measures every thing by an exaҁt Line, and forgives nothing ; pleases himself with himself onely ; the onely Rich, the onely Wise, the onely Free Man, and onely King ; in brief, the onely man that is every thing, but in his own single judgment onely ; that cares not for the Friendship of any man, being himself a friend to no man ; makes no doubt to make the Gods ſtoop to him, and condemns and laughs at the whole Aҁtions of our Life ?

And yet such a Beaſt is this their perfeҁt Wise Man. But tell me pray, if the thing were to be carri'd by most voices,

*He sets up a stony semblance of a man, void of all
sense and common feeling of humanity*

what City would chuse him for its Governour, or what Army desire him for their General ? What Woman would have such a Husband, what Good-fellow such a Guest, or what Servant would either wish or endure such a Master ? Nay, who had not rather have one of the middle sort of Fools, who, being a Fool himself, may the better know how to command or obey Fools ; and who though he please his like, 'tis yet the greater number ; one that is kind to his Wife, merry among his Friends, a Boon Companion, and easie to be liv'd with ; and lastly one that thinks nothing of Humanity should be a stranger to him ? But I am weary of this Wise Man, and therefore I'll proceed to some other advantages.

Go to then. Suppose a man in some lofty high Tower, and that he could look round him, as the Poets say Jupiter was now and then wont. To how many misfortunes would he find the life of man subject ? How miserable, to say no worse, our Birth, how difficult our Education ; to how many wrongs our Childhood expos'd, to what pains our Youth ; how unsupportable our Old-age, and grievous our unavoidable Death ? as also what Troups of Diseases beset us, how many Casualties hang over our Heads, how many Troubles invade us, and how little there is that is not steept in Gall ? to say nothing of those evils one man brings upon another, as Poverty, Imprisonment, Infamy, Dishonesty, Racks, Snares, Treachery, Reproaches, Actions, Deceipts—But I'm got into as endless a work as numbring the Sands—For what offences Mankind have deserv'd these things, or what angry God compell'd 'em to be born into such miseries, is not my present business. Yet he that shall diligently examine it with himself, would he not, think ye, approve the example of the Milesian Virgins, and kill himself ? But who are they that for no other reason but that they were weary of life, have hastned their own Fate ? were they not the next Neighbours to Wisdom ? amongst whom, to say nothing of Diogenes, Xenocrates, Cato, Cassius, Brutus, that Wise Man Chiron, being offer'd Immortality, chose rather to dye than be troubled with the same thing always.

Folly Sweetens Men's Greatest Misfortunes

And now I think ye see what would become of the World if all men should be wise ; to wit 'twere necessary we got another kind of Clay and some better Potter. But I, partly through ignorance, partly unadvisedness, and sometimes through forgetfulness of evil, do now and then so sprinkle pleasure with the hopes of good, and sweeten

So many Nestors everywhere that have scarce left them the shape of a man, stutterers, dotards, toothless, gray-haired, bald

men up in their greatest misfortunes, that they are not willing to leave this life, even then when according to the account of the Destinys this life has left them ; and by how much the less reason they have to live, by so much the more they desire it ; so far are they from being sensible of the least wearisomness of life. Of my gift it is, that ye have so many old Nestors every where, that have scarce left 'em so much as the shape of a Man ; Stutterers, Dotards, Toothless, Gray-hair'd, Bald ; or rather, to use the words of Aristophanes, "Nasty, Crumpt, Miserable, Shrivel'd, Bald, Toothless, and wanting their Baubles" : yet so delighted with life and to be thought young, that one dies his gray hairs ; another covers his baldness with a Periwigg ; another gets a set of new Teeth ; another falls desperately in love with a young Wench, and keeps more flickering about her than a young man would have been asham'd of. For to see such an old crooked piece, with one foot in the grave, to marrie a plump young Wench, and that too without a portion, is so common that men almost expect to be commended for 't.

But the best sport of all is to see our old Women, even dead with age, and such skeletons one would think they had stoln out of their graves, and ever mumbling in their mouths, "Life is sweet"; and as old as they are, still catterwawling, daily plaistering their face, scarce ever from the glasse, gossipping, dancing, and writing Love-letters.

These things are laught at as foolish, as indeed they are ; yet they please themselves, live merrily, swimme in pleasure, and in a word are happy, by my courtesie. But I would have them to whom these things seem ridiculous, to consider with themselves whether it be not better to live so pleasant a life, in such kind of follies, than, as the Proverb goes, " To take a Halter and hang themselves ". Besides though these things may be subject to censure, it concerns not my fools in the least, in as much as they take no notice of it, or if they do, they easily neglect it. If a stone fall upon a man's head, that's evil indeed ; but dishonesty, infamy, villany, ill reports, carrie no more hurt in them than a man is sensible of ; and if a man have no sense of them, they are no longer evils. What art thou the worse if the people hisse at thee, so thou applaud thy self ? And that a man be able to do so, he must ow it only to Folly.

But methinks I hear the Philosophers opposing it, and saying 'tis a miserable thing for a man to be foolish, to erre, mistake, and know nothing truly. Nay rather, this is to be a man. And why they should call it miserable, I see no reason ; forasmuch as we are so born, so bred, so inſtructed, nay, such is the common condition of us all. And nothing can be call'd miserable that suits with its kind, unless perhaps you'l think a man such because he can neither flie with Birds, nor walk on all four with Beaſts, and is not arm'd with Horns as a Bull. For by the same reason he would call the Warlike Horse unfortunate, because he underſtood not Grammar, nor eat Chees-cakes ; and the Bull miserable, because he'd make so ill a Wreſtler. And therefore, as a Horse that has no skill in Grammar is not miserable, no more is man in this respect, for that they agree with his Nature.

Science is the Plague of Mankind

But again, the Virtuosi may say that there was par-ticularly added to Man the knowledge of Sciences, by whose help he might recompence himself in Underſtand-ing for what Nature cut him short in other things. As if this had the leaſt face of truth, that Nature, that was so sollicitously watchful in the production of Gnats, Herbs and Flowers, should have so slept when she made Man, that he should have need to be helpt by Sciences, which that old Devil Theuth, the evil Genius of mankind, firſt invented for his Deſtruction, and are so little conducing to happiness that they rather obſtruct it ; to which purpose

145

they are properly said to be firſt found out, as that wise King in Plato argues touching the invention of Letters.

Sciences therefore crept into the world with other the peſts of mankind, from the same head from whence all other mischiefs spring ; wee'l suppose it Devils, for so the name imports when you call them Dæmons, that is to say, Knowing. For that simple people of the golden Age, being wholly ignorant of every thing call'd Learning, liv'd only by the guidance and dictates of Nature ; for what use of Grammar, where every man spoke the same Language and had no further design than to underſtand one another ? What use of Logick, where there was no bickering about the double-meaning words ? What need of Rhetorick, where there were no Law-suits ? Or to what purpose Laws, where there were no ill manners ? from which without doubt good Laws firſt came. Besides, they were more religious than with an impious curiosity to dive into the secrets of Nature, the dimension of Starrs, the motions, effects, and hidden causes of things ; as believing it a crime for any man to attempt to be wise beyond his condition. And as to the Inquiry of what was beyond Heaven, that madness never came into their heads. But the purity of the golden age declining by degrees, firſt, as I said before, Arts were invented by the evil Genii ; and yet but

For physic, especially as it is now professed by most
men, is nothing but a branch of flattery

few, and those too receiv'd by fewer. After that the Chaldean Superstition and Greek newfangledness, that had little to do, added I know not how many more ; meer torments of Wit, and that so great that even Grammar alone is work enough for any man for his whole life.

Though yet amongst these Sciences those only are in esteem that come nearest to common sense, that is to say, Folly. Divines are half starv'd, Naturalists out of heart, Astrologers laught at, and Logicians slighted ; onely the Physician is worth all the rest. And amongst them too, the more unlearned, impudent, or unadvised he is, the more he is esteem'd, even among Princes. For Physick, especially as it is now profest by most men, is nothing but a branch of Flattery, no less than Rhetorick. Next them, the second place is given to our Law-drivers, if not the first ; whose Profession, though I say it my self, most men laugh at as the Ass of Philosophy ; yet there's scarce any business, either so great or small, but is manag'd by these Asses. These purchase their great Lordships, while in the mean time the Divine, having run through the whole Body of Divinity, sits gnawing a Raddish, and is in continual Warfare with Lice and Fleas.

As therefore those Arts are best that have the nearest Affinity with Folly, so are they most happy of all others that have leaſt commerce with Sciences, and follow the guidance of Nature, who is in no wise imperfeƈt, unless perhaps we endeavour to leap over those bounds she has appointed to us. Nature hates all false-colouring, and is ever beſt where she is leaſt adulterated with Art.

Men Should Follow the Guidance of Nature

Go to then, don't ye find among the several kinds of living Creatures, that they thrive beſt that underſtand no more than what Nature taught them ? What is more prosperous or wonderful than the Bee ? And though they have not the same judgement of sense as other Bodies have, yet wherein hath Architeƈture gone beyond their building of Houses ? What Philosopher ever founded the like Republique ? Whereas the Horse, that comes so near man in underſtanding and is therefore so familiar with him, is also partaker of his misery. For while he thinks it a shame to lose the Race, it often happens that he cracks his wind ; and in the Battel, while he contends for Viƈtory, he's cut down himself, and, together with his Rider, " lies biting the earth " : not to mention those ſtrong Bits, sharp Spurrs, close Stables, Arms, Blows, Rider, and briefly, all that slavery he willingly submits to, while, imitating those men of Valour, he so eagerly ſtrives to be reveng'd of the Enemy. Than which how much more were the life of flies or birds to be wish'd for, who living by the inſtinct of Nature look no further than the present, if yet man would but let 'em alone in 't. And if at any time they chance to be taken, and being shut up in Cages endeavour to imitate our speaking, 'tis ſtrange how they degenerate from their native gaiety. So much better in every respect are the works of Nature than the adulteries of Art.

In like manner I can never sufficiently praise that Pythagoras in a Dung-hill Cock, who being but one had been yet every thing ; a Philosopher, a Man, a Woman, a King, a private man, a Fish, a Horse, a Frog, and I believe too, a Sponge ; and at laſt concluded that no Creature was more miserable than man, for that all other Creatures are content with those bounds that Nature set them, onely Man endeavours to exceed them.

And again, among men he gives the precedency not to the learned or the great, but the Fool. Nor had that Gryllus less wit than Ulysses with his many counsels, who chose rather to lie grunting in a Hog-ſty than be expos'd with t' other to so many hazards. Nor does Homer, that Father of trifles, dissent from me ; who not only call'd all men " wretched and full of calamity ", but often his great pat-

149

tern of Wisedom, Ulysses, " Miserable " ; Paris, Ajax, and
Achilles no where. And why, I pray ? but that, like a cun-
ning fellow and one that was his craft's-master, he did
nothing without the advice of Pallas. In a word he was too
wise, and by that means ran wide of Nature.

As therefore amongst men they are least happy that
study Wisedom, as being in this twice-Fools, that when
they are born men they should yet so far forget their condition as to affect the life of Gods ; and after the Example
of the Gyants, with their Philosophical gimcracks make
a War upon Nature : so they on the other side seem as
little miserable as is possible, who come nearest to Beasts
and never attempt any thing beyond Man. Go to then,
let's try how demonstrable this is ; not by Enthymems or
the imperfect Syllogisms of the Stoicks, but by plain,
downright and ordinary Examples.

And now, by the immortal Gods ! I think nothing more
happy than that generation of men we commonly call
fools, ideots, lack-wits and dolts ; splendid Titles too, as
I conceive 'em. I'le tell ye a thing, which at first perhaps
may seem foolish and absurd, yet nothing more true. And
first they are not afraid of death ; no small evil, by Jupiter !
They are not tormented with the conscience of evil acts ;
not terrify'd with the fables of Ghosts, nor frighted with

Spirits and Goblins. They are not diſtracted with the fear of evils to come, nor the hopes of future good. In short they are not diſturb'd with those thousand of cares to which this life is subject. They are neither modeſt, nor fearful, nor ambitious, nor envious, nor love they any man. And laſtly if they should come nearer even to the very ignorance of Brutes, they could not sin, for so hold the Divines.

And now tell me, thou wise fool, with how many troublesome cares thy mind is continually perplext ; heap together all the discommodities of thy life, and then thou'lt be sensible from how many evils I have delivered my Fools. Add to this that they are not onely merry, play, sing, and laugh themselves, but make mirth where ever they come, a special priviledge it seems the Gods have given 'em to refresh the pensiveness of life. Whence it is, that whereas the world is so differently affected one towards another,— that all men indifferently admit them as their companions, desire, feed, cherish, embrace them, take their parts upon all occasions, and permit 'em without offence to do or say what they liſt. And so little doth every thing desire to hurt them, that even the very Beaſts, by a kind of natural inſtinct of their innocence no doubt, pass by their injuries. For of them it may be truly said that they are consecrate to the Gods, and therefore and not without cause do men have 'em in such esteem.

Why Fools Are in Great Request with Princes

Whence is it else that they are in so great request with Princes, that they can neither eat nor drink, go any whither, or be an hour without them ? Nay, and in some degree they prefer these Fools before their crabbish Wise-men, whom yet they keep about them for State-sake. Nor do I conceive the reason so difficult, or that it should seem strange why they are prefer'd before t' others, for that these wise men speak to Princes about nothing but grave, serious matters, and trusting to their own parts and learning do not fear sometimes " to grate their tender ears with smart truths "; but fools fit 'em with that they most delight in, as jeasts, laughter, abuses of other men, wanton pastimes, and the like.

Again, take notice of this no contemptible blessing which Nature hath giv'n fools, that they are the only plain, honest men and such as speak truth. And what is more commendable than truth ? for though that Proverb of Alcibiades in Plato attributes Truth to Drunkards and Children, yet the praise of it is particularly mine, even from the testimony of Euripides ; amongst whose other things there is extant that his honourable saying concerning us, " A fool speaks foolish things ". For whatever a fool has in his heart, he both shews it in his looks and expresses it in his discourse ; while the wise men's are those two Tongues which the same Euripides mentions, whereof the one speaks truth, the other what they judge most seasonable for the occasion.

These are they " that turn black into white ", blow hot and cold with the same breath, and carry a far different meaning in their Breast from what they feign with their Tongue. Yet in the midst of all their prosperity, Princes in this respect seem to me most unfortunate, because, having no one to tell them truth, they are forc't to rece've flatterers for friends.

But, some one may say, the ears of Princes are strangers to truth, and for this reason they avoid those Wise men, because they fear lest some one more frank than the rest should dare to speak to them things rather true than pleasant ; for so the matter is, that they don't much care for truth. And yet this is found by experience among my Fools, that not onely Truths but even open reproaches are heard with pleasure ; so that the same thing which, if it came from a wise man's mouth might prove a Capital

Crime, spoken by a Fool is receiv'd with delight. For
Truth carries with it a certain peculiar Power of pleasing,
if no Accident fall in to give occasion of offence ; which
faculty the Gods have given onely to Fools. And for the
same reasons is it that Women are so earneſtly delighted
with this kind of Men, as being more propense by Nature
to Pleasure and Toyes. And whatsoever they may happen
to do with them, although sometimes it be of the seriouseſt,
yet they turn it to Jeſt and Laughter ; as that Sexe was
ever quick-witted, especially to colour their own faults.

But to return to the happiness of Fools, who when they
have paſt over this life with a great deal of Pleasantness,
and without so much as the leaſt fear or sense of Death,
they go ſtraight forth into the Elysian Field, to recreate
their Pious and Careless Souls with such Sports as they
us'd here. Let's proceed then, and compare the condition
of any of your Wise Men with that of this Fool. Fancy to
me now some example of Wisdome you'd set up againſt
him ; one that had spent his Childhood and Youth in
learning the Sciences ; and loſt the sweeteſt part of his life
in Watchings, Cares, Studies ; and for the remaining part
of it never so much as taſted the leaſt of pleasure ; ever
sparing, poor, sad, sowre, unjuſt and rigorous to himself,
and troublesome and hateful to others ; broken with Pale-

They go through life with a great deal of pleasantness
and without so much as the least fear of death

ness, Leanness, Crasiness, sore Eyes, and an Old-age and
Death contracted before their time (though yet, what
matter is it, when he dye that never liv'd ?) ; and such is
the Picture of this great Wise Man.

All Madness is not Misfortune

And here again do those Frogs of the Stoicks croak at
me, and say that nothing is more miserable than Madness.
But Folly is the next degree, if not the very thing. For
what else is Madness than for a man to be out of his wits ?
But to let 'em see how they are clean out of the way, with
the Muses' good favour we'll take this Syllogism in pieces.
Subtilly argu'd, I must confess, but as Socrates in Plato
teaches us how by splitting one Venus and one Cupid to
make two of either, in like manner should those Logicians
have done, and distinguisht Madness from Madness, if at
least they would be thought to be well in their wits themselves. For all Madness is not miserable, or Horace had
never call'd his Poetical fury a beloved Madness ; nor
Plato plac'd the Raptures of Poets, Prophets and Lovers
amongst the chiefest Blessings of this Life ; nor that Sybil
in Virgil call'd Æneas's Travels Mad Labours.

But there are two sorts of Madness ; the one that which
the revengeful Furies send privily from Hell, as often

as they let loose their Snakes, and put into men's breasts either the desire of War, or an insatiate thirst after Gold, or some dishonest Love, or Parricide, or Incest, or Sacriledge, or the like Plagues, or when they terrifie some guilty soul with the Conscience of his Crimes ; the other, but nothing like this, that which comes from me, and is of all other things the most desirable ; which happens as oft as some pleasing dotage not onely clears the mind of its troublesome cares, but renders it more jocund. And this was that which, as a special blessing of the Gods, Cicero, writing to his friend Atticus, wisht to himself, that he might be the less sensible of those miseries that then hung over the Common-wealth.

Nor was that Grecian in Horace much wide of it, who was so far mad that he would sit by himself whole daies in the Theatre laughing and clapping his hands, as if he had seen some Tragedy acting, whereas in truth there was nothing presented ; yet in other things a man well enough, pleasant among his Friends, kind to his Wife, and so good a Master to his Servants, that if they had broken the Seal of his Bottle he would not have run mad for 't. But at last, when by the care of his Friends and Physick he was freed from his Distemper, and become his own man again, he thus expostulates with them : "Now, by Pollux, my

Friends, ye have rather kill'd than preserv'd me, in thus forcing me from my pleasure ". By which you see he lik'd it so well that he loſt it againſt his will. And truſt me, I think they were the madder o' th' two, and had the greater need of Hellebore, that should offer to look upon so pleasant a madness as an evil to be remov'd by Physick ; though yet I have not determin'd whether every Diſtemper of the Sense or Underſtanding be to be call'd Madnesse.

For neither he that having weak eyes should take a Mule for an Ass, nor he that should admire an insipid Poem as excellent, would be presently thought mad ; but he that not onely erreth in his senses, but is deceived also in his judgment, and that too more than ordinary and upon all occasions,—he, I muſt confess, would be thought to come very near to it. As if any one hearing an Ass bray should take it for excellent musick, or a Begger conceive himself a King.

And yet this kind of madness, if, as it commonly happens, it turn to pleasure, it brings a great delight not onely to them that are posseſt with it, but to those also that behold it ; though perhaps they may not be altogether so mad as the other, for the Species of this madness is much larger than the people take it to be. For one mad man laughs at another, and beget themselves a mutual pleasure. Nor does it seldom happen, that he that is the more mad, laughs at him that is lesse mad. And in this every man is the more happy, in how many respects the more he is mad ; and if I were judge in the case, he should be rang'd in that Classis of Folly that is peculiarly mine ; which in troth is so large and universal, that I scarce know any one in all mankind that is wise at all hours, or has not some tang or other of madness.

And to this Classis do they appertain that sleight every thing in comparison of hunting, and protest they take an unimaginable pleasure to hear the yell of the Horns and the yelps of the Hounds, and I believe could pick somewhat extraordinary out of their very excrement. And then what pleasure they take to see a Buck or the like unlac'd ? Let ordinary fellows cut up an Ox or a Weather, 'twere a crime to have this done by any thing less than a Gentleman ! who with his Hat off, on his bare knees, and a Cuttoe for that purpose (for every Sword or Knife is not allowable), with a curious superstition and certain postures, layes open the several parts in their respective order ; while they that hemm him in admire it with silence, as some new religious Ceremony, though perhaps they have seen it an hundred times before. And if any of 'em chance to get the least piece of 't, he presently thinks himself no small Gentleman. In all which they drive at nothing more than to become Beasts themselves, while yet they imagin they live the life of Princes.

And next these may be reckon'd those that have such an itch of Building; one while changing Rounds into Squares, and presently again Squares into Rounds; never knowing either measure or end, till at last, reduc'd to the utmost poverty, there remains not to them so much as a place where they may lay their head, or wherewith to fill their bellyes. And why all this? but that they may pass over a few years in feeding their foolish fancies.

And, in my opinion, next these may be reckon'd such as with their new inventions and occult arts undertake to change the forms of things, and hunt all about after a certain fifth Essence; Men so bewitcht with this present hope that it never repents them of their pains or expence, but are ever contriving how they may cheat themselves; till, having spent all, there is not enough left them to provide another furnace. And yet they have not done dreaming these their pleasant Dreams, but encourage others, as much as in them lies, to the same Happiness. And at last, when they are quite loſt in all their Expectations, they chear up themselves with this Sentence, " In great things the very attempt is enough " ; and then complain of the shortness of man's life, that is not sufficient for so great an Undertaking.

And then for Gameſters, I am a little doubtful whether they are to be admitted into our Colledge ; and yet 'tis a foolish and ridiculous sight to see some addicted so to 't, that they can no sooner hear the ratling of the Dice but their heart leaps and dances again. And then when time after time they are so far drawn on with the hopes of winning that they have made shipwrack of all, and having split their Ship on that Rock of Dice, no less terrible than the Bishop and 's Clerks, scarce got alive to shore, they chuse rather to cheat any man of their juſt Debts than not pay the money they loſt, leſt otherwise, forsooth, they be thought no men of their words. Again what is it, I pray, to see old fellows and half blind to play with Spectacles ? Nay and when a juſtly-deserv'd Gout has knotted their Knuckles, to hire a Caſter, or one that may put the Dice in the Box for them ? A pleasant thing, I muſt confess, did it not for the moſt part end in quarrels, and therefore belongs rather to the Furies than Me.

On Those who have Confidence in Magical Charms

But there is no doubt but that that kind of men are wholly ours, who love to hear or tell feign'd Miracles and strange lyes, and are never weary of any Tale, though never so long, so it be of Ghosts, Spirits, Goblings, Devils, or the like ; which the farther they are from truth, the more readily they are believ'd and the more do they tickle their itching ears. And these serve not only to pass away time, but bring profit, especially to Masse Priests and Pardoners.

And next to these are they that have gotten a foolish but pleasant perswasion, that if they can but see a Wodden or painted Polypheme Christopher, they shall not die that day ; or do but salute a carv'd-Barbara, in the usual set Form, that he shall return safe from Battail ; or make his application to Erasmus on certain days with some small Wax Candles and proper Prayers, that he shall quickly be rich. Nay, they have gotten an Hercules, another Hippolytus, and a St. George, whose Horse most religiously set out with Trappings and Bosses there wants little but they worship ; however, they endeavour to make him their friend by some Present or other ; and to swear by his Master's Brazen Helmet is an Oath for a Prince.

Or what should I say of them that hugg themselves with their counterfeit Pardons; that have measur'd Purgatory by an Hour-glass, and can without the least mistake demonstrate its Ages, Years, Moneths, Days, Hours, Minutes, and Seconds, as it were in a Mathematical Table? Or what of those who, having confidence in certain Magical charms and short Prayers invented by some pious Impostour, either for his Soul's health or profit's sake, promise to themselves every thing: Wealth, Honour, Pleasure, Plenty, good Health, long Life, lively Old-age, and the next place to Christ in the other World, which yet they desire may not happen too soon, that is to say before the pleasures of this life have left them?

And now suppose some Merchant, Souldier, or Judge, out of so many Rapines, parts with some small piece of money. He straight conceives all that sink of his whole life quite cleans'd; so many Perjuries, so many Lusts, so many Debaucheries, so many Contentions, so many Murders, so many Deceipts, so many breaches of Trust, so many Treacheries bought off, as it were by compact; and so bought off that they may begin upon a new score. But what is more foolish than those, or rather more happy, who daily reciting those seven verses of the Psalms promise to

themselves more than the top of Felicity ? which Magical
verses some Devil or other, a merry one without doubt
but more a Blab of his Tongue than crafty, is believ'd to
have discover'd to St. Bernard, but not without a Trick.
And these are so foolish that I am half asham'd of 'em my
self, and yet they are approv'd, and that not onely by the
common people, but even the Professors of Religion.

And what, are not they also almoſt the same where
several Countryes avouch to themselves their peculiar
Saint, and as every one of them has his particular gift, so
also his particular Form of Worship ? As, one is good
for the Tooth-ach ; another, for Groaning-women ; a
third, for Stollen Goods ; a fourth, for making a Voyage
Prosperous ; and a fifth, to cure Sheep of the Rot ; and so
of the reſt, for it would be too tedious to run over all. And
some there are that are good for more things than one ;
but chiefly, the Virgin Mother, to whom the common
people do in a manner attribute more than to the Son.

Yet what do they beg of these Saints but what belongs
to Folly ? To examine it a little. Among all those offerings
which are so frequently hung up in Churches, nay up
to the very Roof of some of 'em, did you ever see the leaſt
acknowledgment from any one that had left his Folly, or
grown a Hair's-breadth the wiser ? One scapes a Ship-

wrack, and gets safe to Shore. Another, run through in a
Duel, recovers. Another, while the reſt were fighting, ran
out of the Field, no less luckily than valiantly. Another,
condemn'd to be hang'd, by the favour of some Saint or
other, a friend to Thieves, got off himself by impeaching
his fellows. Another escap'd by breaking Prison. Another
recover'd from his Feaver in spight of his Phyſitian. Another's poison turning to a loosness prov'd his Remedy
rather than Death ; and that to his Wife's no small sorrow,
in that she loſt both her labour and her charge. Another's
Cart broke, and he sav'd his Horses. Another preserv'd
from the fall of a House. All these hang up their Tablets,
but no one gives thanks for his recovery from Folly ; so
sweet a thing it is not to be Wise, that on the contrary men
rather pray againſt any thing than Folly.

But why do I lanch out into this Ocean of Superſtitions ?
Had I an hundred Tongues, as many Mouthes, and a
Voice never so ſtrong, yet were I not able to run over the
several sorts of Fools, or all the names of Folly ; so thick
do they swarm every where. And yet our Prieſts make
no scruple to receive and cherish 'em, as proper inſtruments
of profit ; whereas if some scurvy Wise fellow should ſtep
up, and speak things as they are, as, To live well is the
way to dye well ; The beſt way to get quit of sin is to add

Another, run through in a duel, recovers

to the money thou giv'st, the Hatred of sin, Tears, Watchings, Prayers, Fastings, and amendment of life ; Such or
such a Saint will favour thee, if thou imitatest his life ;
—these, I say, and the like, should this Wise man chat to
the people, from what happiness into how great troubles
would he draw 'em ?

Of this Colledge also are they who in their lifetime
appoint with what solemnity they'll be buried, and par-
ticularly set down how many Torches, how many Mourn-
ers, how many Singers, how many Alms-men they will
have at it ; as if any sense of it could come to them, or that
it were a shame to them that their Corpse were not hon-
ourably interr'd ; so curious are they herein, as if, like
the Ædiles of old, these were to present some Shews or
Banquet to the people.

How much Satisfaction Self-Love Begets Everywhere

And though I am in hast, yet I cannot yet pass by them
who, though they differ nothing from the meanest Cobler,
yet 'tis scarcely credible how they flatter themselves with
the empty Title of Nobility. One derives his Pedegree
from Æneas, another from Brutus, a third from the Star
by the Tail of Ursa Major. They shew you on every side

the Statues and Pictures of their Ancestours; run over their great Grandfathers and great great Grandfathers of both Lines, and the Antient Matches of their Families; when themselves yet are but once remov'd from a Statue, if not worse than those trifles they boast of. And yet by means of this pleasant self-love they live a happy life. Nor are they less Fools who admire these Beasts as if they were Gods.

But what do I speak of any one or t' other particular kind of men, as if this self-Love had not the same effect every where, and render'd most men superabundantly happy? As when a fellow, more deform'd than a Baboon, shall believe himself handsomer than Homer's Nireus. Another, as soon as he can draw two or three lines with a Compass, presently think himself an Euclid. A third, that understands Musick no more than my Horse, and for his voice as hoarse as a Dunghill-Cock, shall yet conceive himself another Hermogenes. But of all madness that's the most pleasant, when a man, seeing another any way excellent in what he pretends to himself, makes his boasts of it as confidently as if it were his own. And such was that rich fellow in Seneca, who when ever he told a story had his servants at his elbow to prompt him the names; and to that height had they flatter'd him, that he did not ques-

tion but he might venture a rubber at cuffs, a man otherwise so weak he could scarce ſtand, onely presuming on
this, that he had a company of ſturdy servants about him.

Or to what purpose is it I should mind ye of our professors of Arts ? Forasmuch as this Self-love is so natural
to them all, that they had rather part with their Father's
land than their foolish Opinions ; but chiefly Players,
Fidlers, Orators, and Poets, of which the more ignorant
each of them is, the more insolently he pleases himself,
that is to say Vaunts and Spreads out his Plumes. And
like lips find like Lettice ; nay, the more foolish any thing
is, the more 'tis admir'd ; the greater number being ever
tickled at the worſt things, because, as I said before, moſt
men are so subject to Folly. And therefore if the more
foolish a man is, the more he pleases himself and is
admir'd by others, to what purpose should he beat his
brains about true knowledg, which firſt will coſt him
dear, and next render him the more troublesome and less
confident, and, laſtly, please onely a few ?

And now I consider it, Nature has planted, not onely
in particular men but even in every Nation, and scarce
any City is there without it, a kind of common self-love.
And hence is it that the English, besides other things,
particularly challenge to themselves Beauty, Musick, and

Feasting. The Scots are proud of their Nobility, Alliance to the Crown, and Logical Subtilties. The French think themselves the onely well-bred men. The Parisians, excluding all others, arrogate to themselves the onely knowledg of Divinity. The Italians affirm they are the onely Masters of good Letters and Eloquence, and flatter themselves on this account, that of all others they onely are not barbarous. In which kind of happiness those of Rome claim the first place, still dreaming to themselves of somewhat, I know not what, of old Rome. The Venetians fancy themselves happy in the opinion of their Nobility. The Greeks, as if they were the onely Authors of Sciences, swell themselves with the Titles of the Antient Heroes. The Turk, and all that sink of the truly barbarous, challenge to themselves the onely glory of Religion, and laugh at Christians as superstitious. And much more pleasantly the Jews expect to this day the coming of the Messias, and so obstinately contend for their Law of Moses. The Spaniards give place to none in the reputation of Souldiery. The Germans pride themselves in their Talness of Stature and skill in Magick.

And, not to instance in every particular, you see, I conceive, how much satisfaction this Self-love, who has a Sister also not unlike her self call'd Flattery, begets

The Italians affirm they are the only masters of elo-
quence, and the Turks challenge to themselves the
only glory of religion

every where ; for Self-love is no more than the soothing
of a man's self, which, done to another, is flattery. And
though perhaps at this day it may be thought infamous,
yet it is so only with them that are more taken with words
than things. They think truth is inconsistent with flattery ;
but that it is much otherwise we may learn from the
examples of brute Beasts. What more fawning than a
Dog ? and yet what more trusty ? What has more of
those little tricks than a Squirrel ? and yet what more
loving to man ? Unless, perhaps you'll say, Men had
better converse with fierce Lions, merciless Tigers, and
furious Leopards. For that flattery is the most pernicious
of all things, by means of which some treacherous persons and mockers have run the credulous into such mischief.

But this of mine proceeds from a certain gentleness
and uprightness of mind, and comes nearer to Vertue
than its opposite, Austerity, or a Morose and troublesome peevishness, as Horace calls it. This supports the
dejected, relieves the distressed, encourages the fainting,
awakens the stupid, refreshes the sick, supples the untract-
able, joyns loves together, and keeps them so joyn'd. It
entices children to take their learning, makes old men
frolick, and, under the colour of praise, does without

offence both tell Princes their faults and shew them the way to amend 'em. In short, it makes every man the more jocund and acceptable to himself, which is the chiefeſt point of felicity. Agen, what is more friendly than when two horses scrub one another ? And to say nothing of it, that it's a main part of that fam'd eloquence, the better part of Physick, and the onely thing in Poetry ; 'tis the delight and relish of all humane Society.

But 'tis a sad thing, they say, to be miſtaken. Nay rather, he is moſt miserable that is not so. For they are quite beside the mark that place the Happiness of men in Things themselves, since it onely depends upon Opinion. For so great is the obscurity and variety of humane affairs, that nothing can be clearly known, as it is truly said by our Academicks, the leaſt insolent of all the Philosophers ; or if it could, it would but obſtruct the pleasure of life. Laſtly, the mind of man is so fram'd that it is rather taken with false colours than truth ; of which if any one has a mind to make the experiment, let him go to Church and hear Sermons, in which if there be any thing serious deliver'd, the Auditory is either asleep, yawning, or weary of 't ; but if the Preacher—pardon my miſtake, I would have said Declaimer—, as too often it happens, fall but into an old Wife's ſtory, they 're pres-

For suppose a man were eating rotten stockfish and
yet believed it a dish for the gods

ently awake, prick up their ears and gape after it. In like manner, if there be any Poetical Saint, or one of whom there goes more ſtories than ordinary, as for example, a George, a Chriſtopher, or a Barbara, you shall see him more religiously worshipp'd than Peter, Paul, or even Chriſt himself. But these things are not for this place.

At How Cheap a Rate is this Happiness Purchased

And now at how cheap a rate is this happiness purchaſt ! Forasmuch as to the thing it self a man's whole endeavour is requir'd, be it never so inconsiderable ; but the opinion of it is easily taken up, which yet conduceth as much or more to happiness. For suppose a man were eating rotten Stockfish, the very smell of which would choak another, and yet believ'd it a dish for the Gods, what difference is there as to his happiness ? Whereas on the contrary, if another's ſtomack should turn at a Sturgion, wherein, I pray, is he happier than t' other ? If a man have a crooked, ill-favour'd Wife, who yet in his Eye may ſtand in competition with Venus, is it not the same as if she were truly beautiful ? Or if seeing an ugly, ill-painted piece, he should admire the work as believing it some great Maſter's hand, were he not much happier, think ye, than they that buy such things at vaſt rates, and yet perhaps reap less pleasure from 'em than t' other ?

I know one of my name that gave his new marri'd Wife some counterfeit Jewels, and, as he was a pleasant Droll, perswaded her that they were not onely right, but of an ineſtimable price ; and what difference, I pray, to her, that was as well pleas'd and contented with Glass, and kept it as warily as if 't 'ad been a treasure ? In the mean time the Husband sav'd his money, and had this advantage of her folly, that he oblig'd her as much as if he had bought 'em at a great rate. Or what difference, think ye, between those in Plato's imaginary Cave, that ſtand gaping at the Shadows and Figures of things, so they please themselves and have no need to wish ; and that Wise Man, who, being got loose from 'em, sees things truly as they are ? Whereas that Cobler in Lucian, if he might always have continu'd his Golden Dreams, he would never have desir'd any other happiness.

So then there is no difference ; or, if there be, the Fools ha' the 'vantage : firſt, in that their happiness coſts them leaſt, that is to say, onely some small perswasion ; next, that they enjoy it in common. And the possession of no good can be delightful without a companion. For who does not know what a dearth there is of Wise men, if yet any one be to be found? and though the Greeks for these so many ages have accounted upon seaven only, yet so help me Hercules, do but examine 'em narrowly, and I'll be hang'd if ye find one half-witted fellow, nay or so much as one quarter of a Wise man, amongst 'em all.

Why Should Folly Envy the Rest of the Gods?

For whereas among the many praises of Bacchus they reckon this the chief, that he washeth away cares, and that too in an instant; do but sleep off his weak spirits, and they come on agen, as we say, on horseback. But how much larger and more present is the benefit ye receive by me, since, as it were with a perpetual drunkenness, I fill your minds with Mirth, Fancies and Jollities, and that too without any trouble? Nor is there any man living whom I let be without it; whereas the gifts of the Gods are scambled, some to one and some to another.

The sprightly delicious Wine that drives away cares and leaves such a Flavour behind it, grows not every where. Beauty, the gift of Venus, happens to few; and to fewer gives Mercury Eloquence. Hercules makes not every one rich. Homer's Jupiter bestows not Empire on all men. Mars oftentimes favours neither side. Many re-

173

turn sad from Apollo's Oracle. Phoebus sometimes shoots a Plague amongst us. Neptune drowns more than he saves : to say nothing of those mischievous Gods, Plutoes, Ates, Punishments, Feavours and the like, not Gods but Executioners.

I am that only Folly that so readily and indifferently bestow my benefits on all. Nor do I look to be entreated, or am I subject to take pett, and require an expiatory sacrifice if some Ceremony be omitted. Nor do I beat heaven and earth together, if, when the rest of the Gods are invited, I am past by or not admitted to the steam of their Sacrifices. For the rest of the Gods are so curious in this point, that such an omission may chance to spoil a man's business ; and therefore one had as good ev'n let 'em alone as worship 'em : just like some men, who are so hard to please, and withall so ready to do mischief, that 'tis better be a stranger than have any familiarity with 'em.

But no man, you'll say, ever sacrific'd to Folly, or built me a Temple. And troth, as I said before, I cannot but wonder at the ingratitude ; yet because I am easie to be entreated, I take this also in good part, though truelie I can scarce request it. For why should I require Incense, Wafers, a Goat or Sow, when all men pay me that worship every where, which is so much approv'd even by our very

Divines ? Unless perhaps I should envy Diana, that her Sacrifices are mingled with Humane blood. Then do I conceive my self moſt religiouslie worshipp'd, when every where, as 'tis generally done, men embrace me in their Minds, express me in their Manners, and represent me in their Lives ; which worship of the Saints is not so ordinary among Chriſtians. How many are there that burn Candles to the Virgin Mother, and that too at noon day, when there 's no need of 'em ! But how few are there that ſtudie to imitate her in pureness of Life, Humility and love of Heavenlie things, which is the true worship and moſt acceptable to Heaven !

Besides why should I desire a Temple, when the whole world is my Temple, and I'm deceiv'd or 'tis a goodly one ? Nor can I want Prieſts, but in a Land where there are no men. Nor am I yet so foolish as to require Statues or painted Images, which do often obſtruct my Worship, since among the ſtupid and grosſ multitude those Figures are worshipt for the Saints themselves. And so it would fare with me, as it doth with them that are turn'd out of doors by their Subſtitutes. No, I have Statues enough, and as many as there are Men ; every one bearing my lively Resemblance in his Face, how unwilling so ever he be to the contrary.

And therefore there is no reason why I should envie the rest of the Gods, if in particular places they have their particular worship, and that too on set-days— as Phoebus at Rhodes; at Cyprus, Venus; at Argos, Juno; at Athens, Minerva; in Olympus, Jupiter; at Tarentum, Neptune; and near the Hellespont, Priapus— ; as long as the World in general performs me every day much better Sacrifices.

On the Follies and Madnesses of the Common People

Wherein notwithstanding if I shall seem to any one to have spoken more boldlie than trulie, let us, if ye please, look a little into the lives of men, and it will easily appear not onely how much they owe to me, but how much they esteem me even from the highest to the lowest. And yet we will not run over the lives of everie one, for that would be too long; but onelie some few of the great ones, from whence we shall easilie conjecture the rest.

For to what purpose is it to say any thing of the common people, who without dispute are whollie mine? For they abound every where with so many several sorts of Folly, and are everie day so busie in inventing new, that a thousand Democriti are too few for so general a laughter,

And another spends all he can on his belly to be the more hungry after it, while still another wastes all his time on sleep

though there were another Democritus to laugh at them too. 'Tis almost incredible what Sport and Pastime they dailie make the Gods ; for though they set aside their sober forenoon hours to dispatch business and receive prayers, yet when they begin to be well whitled with Nectar, and cannot think of anything that's serious, they get 'em up into some part of Heaven that has better prospect than other, and thence look down upon the actions of men. Nor is there anie thing that pleases 'em better. Good, good ! what an excellent sight 'tis ! How many several Hurlie-burlies of Fools ! for I my self sometimes sit among those Poetical Gods.

Here's one desperatelie in love with a young Wench, and the more she sleights him the more outragiouslie he loves her. Another marries a woman's money, not her self. Another's jealousie keeps more eyes on her than Argos. Another becomes a Mourner, and how foolishlie he carries it ! nay, hires others to bear him companie, to make it more ridiculous. Another weeps over his Mother in Law's Grave. Another spends all he can rap and run on his Bellie, to be the more hungry after it. Another thinks there is no happiness but in sleep and idleness. Another turmoils himself about other men's business, and neglects his own. Another thinks himself rich in taking

up moneys and changing Securities, as we say borrow-
ing of Peter to pay Paul, and in a short time becomes
bankrupt. Another ſtarves himself to enrich his Heir.
Another for a small and incertain gain exposes his life to
the casualties of Seas and Winds, which yet no money can
reſtore. Another had rather get Riches by War than live
peaceably at home.

And some there are that think them easieſt attain'd by
courting old childless men with Presents; and others
again by making rich old women believe they love
'm; both which afford the Gods most excellent paſtime,
to see them cheated by those persons they thought to
have over-cach't. But the moſt foolish and baseſt of all
others are our Merchants, to wit such as venture on
every thing be it never so dishoneſt, and manage it no
better; who though they lie by no allowance, swear and
forswear, ſteal, cozen, and cheat, yet shufle themselves
into the firſt rank, and all because they have Gold Rings
on their Fingers. Nor are they without their flattering
Friers that admire them and give 'em openly the title of
Honourable, in hopes, no doubt, to get some small snip
of 't themselves.

There are also a kind of Pythagoreans, with whom all
things are so common, that if they get any thing under

Surrounded by a great swarm of gnats and flies quar-
relling among themselves, fighting, snatching,
playing and wantoning

their Cloaks, they make no more scruple of carrying it away than if 'twere their own by inheritance. There are others too that are onely rich in conceit, and while they fancie to themselves pleasant dreams, conceive that enough to make them happy. Some desire to be accounted wealthy abroad, and are yet ready to ſtarve at home. One makes what haſte he can to set all going, and another rakes it together by right or wrong. This man is ever labouring for publick honours; and another lies sleeping in a Chimney-corner. A great many undertake endless Suites, and outvie one another who shall moſt enrich the Delatory Judge or Corrupt Advocate. One is all for Innovations; and another for some great-he-knows-not-what. Another leaves his Wife and Children at home, and goes to Jerusalem, Rome, or in Pilgrimage to St. James's, where he has no business.

In short, if a man like Menippus of old could look down from the Moon, and behold those innumerable rufflings of Mankind, he would think he saw a swarm of Flies and Gnats quarrelling among themselves, fighting, laying Traps for one another, snatching, playing, wantoning, growing up, falling, and dying. Nor is it to be believ'd what ſtir, what broils this little creature raiseth, and yet in how short a time it comes to nothing its self; while

sometimes War, othertimes Peſtilence, sweeps off many
thousands of 'em together.

The Pleasant Madness of the Learned Profession

But let me be moſt foolish my self, and one whom
Democritus may not onely laugh at but flout, if I go one
foot further in the discovery of the Follies and Madnesses
of the common people. I'll betake me to them that carry
the reputation of Wise men, and hunt after that golden
Bough, as says the Proverb. Amongſt whom the Grammarians hold the firſt place, a generation of men than
whom nothing would be more miserable, nothing more
perplext, nothing more hated of the Gods, did not I allay
the troubles of that pittiful Profession with a certain kind
of pleasant madness. For they are not onely subje∂t to
those five curses with which Homer begins his Iliads, as
says the Greek Epigramme, but six hundred; as being
ever hunger-ſtarv'd, and slovens in their Schools—Schools,
did I say ? Nay, rather Cloiſters, Bridwells or Slaughter-
houses—, grown old among a company of boyes, deaf
with their noise, and pin'd away with ſtench and naſtiness.
And yet by my courtesie it is that they think themselves
the moſt excellent of all men ; so greatly do they please

themselves in frighting a company of fearful boyes, with a thundring voice and big looks; tormenting them with Ferules, Rods, and Whips; and, laying about 'em without fear or wit, imitate the Ass in the Lion's skin. In the mean time all that naſtiness seems absolute Spruceness, that Stench a Perfume, and that miserable slaverie a Kingdom, and such too as they would not change their Tyrannie for Phalaris' or Dionysius's Empire.

Nor are they less happy in that new Opinion they have taken up of being learned; for whereas most of 'em beat into boys' heads nothing but foolish Toyes, yet, ye good Gods! what Palemon, what Donatus, do they not scorn in comparison of themselves? And so, I know not by what tricks, they bring it about that to their boys' foolish Mothers and dolt-headed Fathers they pass for such as they fancy themselves. Add to this that other pleasure of theirs, that if any of 'em happen to find out who was Anchises's Mother, or pick out of some worm-eaten Manuscript a word not commonly known, as suppose it Bubsequa for a Cowheard, Bovinator for a Wrangler, Manticulator for a Cutpurse; or dig up the ruines of some ancient Monument, with the letters half eaten out; O Jupiter! what towrings! what triumphs! what commendations! as if they had conquer'd Africa, or **taken in** Babylon.

But what of this when they give up and down their foolish insipid verses, and there wants not others that admire 'em as much? They believe presently that Virgil's soul is transmigrated into them! But nothing like this, when with mutual complements they praise, admire and claw one another. Whereas if another do but slip a word, and one more quick-sighted than the rest discover it by accident, O Hercules! what uproars, what bickerings, what taunts, what invectives! If I lye, let me have the ill will of all the Grammarians. I knew in my time one of many Arts, a Grecian, a Latinist, a Mathematician, a Philosopher, a Physitian, a Man master of 'em all, and sixty years of age, who, laying by all the rest, perplext and tormented himself for above twenty years in the study of Grammar; fully reckoning himself a Prince if he might but live so long till he could certainly determine how the Eight parts of Speech were to be distinguisht, which none of the Greeks or Latines had yet fully clear'd: as if it were a matter to be decided by the Sword, if a man made an Adverb of a Conjunction.

And for this cause is it that we have as many Grammars as Grammarians; nay more, forasmuch **as my** friend

The poets not only try to assure themselves of immortality and a life like the gods but also promise it to others

Aldus has giv'n us above five, not passing by any kind of Grammar, how barbarously or tediously soever compil'd, which he has not turn'd over and examin'd ; envying every man's attempts in this kind, how foolish so ever, and desperately concern'd for fear another should forestall him of his glory, and the labours of so many years perish. And now, whether had you rather call this Madness or Folly ? It is no great matter to me whether, so long as ye confess it is by my means that a creature, otherwise the most miserable of all others, is rais'd to that height of felicity that he has no desire to change his condition with the King of Persia.

The Poets, I must confess, are not altogether so much beholding to me, though 'tis agreed of all hands they are of my partie too ; because they are a free kind of people, not restrain'd or limited to any thing, and all their studies aim at nothing more than to tickle the ears of fools with meer trifles and ridiculous fables. And yet they are so bold upon 't, that you'll scarce believe how they not onely assure themselves of immortality and a life like the Gods, but promise it to others too. And to this order, before all others, Self-love and Flattery are more peculiarly appendant ; nor am I worshipt by any sort of men with more plainness or greater constancy.

183

And then, for the Rhetoricians, though they now and then shuffle and cut with the Philosopher, yet that these two are of my factions also, though many other Arguments might be produc'd, this clearly evinces it ; that besides their other trifles, they have written so much and so exquisitely of Fooling. And so, who ever he were that writ of the Art of Rhetorick to Herennius, he reckons Folly as a species of wit. And Quintilian, the Soveraign of this Order, has a Chapter touching Laughter more prolixe than an Iliad. In fine, they attribute so much to Folly, that what many times cannot be clear'd with the best Arguments, is yet now and then put off with a jest : unless, perhaps you'll say, 'tis no part of Folly to provoke laughter, and that artificially.

Of the same batch also are they that hunt after immortality of Fame by setting out Books. Of whom, though all of 'em are endebted to me, yet in the first place are they that nothing but daub Paper with their empty Toyes. For they that write learnedly to the understanding of a few Scholers, and refuse not to stand the test of a Persius or Laelius, seem to me rather to be pittied than happy, as persons that are ever tormenting themselves ; Adding, Changing, Putting in, Blotting out, Revising, Reprinting, showing 't to friends, and nine years in correcting, yet never fully satisfied ; at so great a rate do they purchase this vain reward, to wit, Praise, and that too of a very few, with so many watchings, so much sweat, so much vexation and loss of sleep, the most pretious of all things. Add to this the waste of health, spoil of complexion, weakness of eyes or rather blindness, poverty, envie, abstinence from pleasure, over-hasty Old-age, untimely death, and the like ; so highly does this Wise man value the approbation of one or two blear-ey'd fellows.

But how much happier is this my Writer's dotage, who never studies for any thing, but puts in writing what ever he pleases or what comes first in his head, though it be but his dreams ; and all this with small waste of Paper, as well knowing that the vainer those Trifles are, the higher esteem they will have with the greater number, that is to say all the fools and unlearned. And what matter is it to sleight those few learned, if yet they ever read them ? Or of what authority will the censure of so few Wise men be against so great a Cloud of Gainsayers ?

But they are the wiser that put out other men's works for their own, and transfer that glory which others with great pains have obtain'd to themselves ; relying on this, that they conceive, though it should so happen that their theft be never so plainly detected, that yet they should enjoy the pleasure of it for the present. And 'tis worth one's while to consider how they please themselves when they are applauded by the common people, pointed at in a Croud, "This is that excellent person"; lie on Booksellers' ſtalls ; and in the top of every Page have three hard words read, but chiefly Exotick, and next degree to conjuring ; which, by the immortal Gods ! what are they but meer words ?

And agen, if ye consider the world, by how few understood, and prais'd by fewer ! for even amongſt the unlearned there are different palates. Or what is it that their own very names are often conterfeit, or borrow'd from some Books of the Antients ? When one ſtiles himself Telemachus, another Sthenelus, a third Laertes, a fourth Polycrates, a fifth Thrasymachus. So that there is no difference whether they Title their Books with the "Tale of a Tub ", or, according to the Philosophers, by Alpha, Beta.

But the moſt pleasant of all is to see them praise one another with Reciprocal Epiſtles, Verses, and Encomiums ; Fools their fellow-Fools, and Dunces their brother Dunces. This, in t' other's opinion, is an absolute Alcaeus ; and the other, in his, a very Callimachus. He looks upon Tully as nothing to t' other, and t' other again pronounces

How pleased they are when they are applauded by the common people and pointed at in a crowd

him more learned than Plato. And sometimes too they
pick out their Antagonist, and think to raise themselves
a Fame by writing one against t' other ; while the giddy
multitude are so long divided to whether o' th' two they
shall determine the Victory, till each goes off Conqueror,
and, as if he had done some great Action, fancies himself a Triumph.

And now Wise Men laugh at these things as foolish,
as indeed they are. Who denies it ? Yet in the mean time,
such is my kindness to them, they live a merry life, and
would not change their imaginary Triumphs, no, not with
the Scipioes. While yet those Learned men, though they
laugh their fill and reap the benefit of t' others' Folly, cannot without ingratitude denie but that even they too are
not a little beholding to me themselves.

And amongst them our Advocates challenge the first
place, nor is there anie sort of people that please themselves like them : for while they dailie roul Sisyphus his
stone ; and quote ye a thousand cases, as it were in a
breath, no matter how little to the purpose ; and heap
Glosses upon Glosses, and Opinions on the neck of
Opinions ; they bring it at last to this pass, that that
studie of all other seems the most difficult. Add to these,
our Logicians and Sophisters, a generation of men more

pratling than an Echo, and the worſt of 'em able to out-
chat an hundred of the beſt pickt Gossips. And yet their
condition would be much better were they onely full of
words, and not so given to scolding, that they moſt obſti-
natelie hack and hew one another about a matter of
nothing, and make such a sputter about Terms and
words, till they have quite loſt the Sense. And yet they
are so happy in the good opinion of themselves, that as
soon as they are furnisht with two or three Syllogisms,
they dare boldly enter the Liſts againſt any Man upon any
Point ; as not doubting but to run him down with noise,
though the Opponent were another Stentor.

And next these come our Philosophers, so much rever-
enc'd for their Fur'd Gowns and Starcht Beards, that they
look upon themselves as the onely Wise Men, and all
others as Shadows. And yet how pleasantly do they dote
while they frame in their heads innumerable worlds ;
measure out the Sun, the Moon, the Stars, nay and Heaven
it self, as it were with a pair of Compasses ; lay down the
Causes of Lightning, Winds, Eclipses, and other the like
Inexplicable Matters ; and all this too without the leaſt
doubting, as if they were Nature's Secretaries, or dropt
down among us from the Council of the Gods ; while in
the mean time Nature laughs at them and all their blind

How pleasantly do they dote when they frame in their heads innumerable worlds; measure out the sun, the moon, the stars, nay and Heaven itself

conjectures. For, that they know nothing, even this is a sufficient Argument, that they do n't agree amongst themselves, and are so indemonstrable as to others touching every particular.

These, though they have not the least degree of knowledge, profess yet that they have master'd all ; nay, though they neither know themselves, nor perceive a Ditch or Block that lies in their way, for that perhaps most of them are half blind, or their wits a wooll-gathering, yet give out that they have discovr'd Ideas, Universalities, separated Forms, first Matters, Quiddities, Ecceities, Formalities, and the like stuff ; things so thin and bodiless, that I believe even Lynceus himself were not able to perceive 'em. But then chiefly do they disdain the unhallow'd Croud, as often as with their Triangles, Quadrangles, Circles and the like Mathematical Devices, more confounded than a Labyrinth, and Letters dispos'd one against t' other, as it were in Battle-Array, they cast a mist before the eyes of the ignorant. Nor is there wanting of this kind some that pretend to foretell things by the Stars, and make promises of Miracles beyond all things of South-saying, and are so fortunate as to meet with people that believe 'em.

DESIDERIUS ERASMUS

Now Watch Our Great Illuminated Divines

But perhaps I had better pass over our Divines in silence and not ſtir this Pool, or touch this fair but un-savoury Plant; as a kind of men that are supercilious beyond comparison, and to that too, implacable; leſt set-ting 'em about my ears, they attaque me by Troops, and force me to a Recantation-Sermon, which if I refuse, they ſtreight pronounce me an Heretick. For this is the Thunder-bolt with which they fright those whom they are resolv'd not to favour. And truly, though there are few others that less willingly acknowledge the kindnesses I have done them, yet even these too ſtand faſt bound to me upon no ordinary accounts; whilſt being happy in their own Opinion, and as if they dwelt in the third Heaven, they look with Haughtiness on all others as poor creeping things, and could almoſt find in their hearts to pitie 'em; whilſt hedg'd in with so many Magiſterial Defi-nitions, Conclusions, Corollaries, Propositions Explicit and Implicit, they abound with so many ſtarting-holes, that Vulcan's Net cannot hold 'em so faſt, but they'll slip through with their diſtinctions; with which they so easily cut all knots asunder that a Hatchet could not have done

it better, so plentiful are they in their new-found Words
and prodigious Terms. Besides, whilſt they explicate the
moſt hidden Myſteries according to their own fancie :—as,
how the World was firſt made ; how Original Sin is deriv'd
to Poſterity ; in what manner, how much room, and how
long time, Chriſt lay in the Virgin's Womb ; how Acci-
dents subsiſt in the Euchariſt without their Subject.

But these are common and threadbare ; these are worthy
of our great and illuminated Divines, as the world calls
'em ! At these, if ever they fall a thwart 'em, they prick
up :—as, whether there was any inſtant of time in the
generation of the Second Person ; whether there be more
than one Filiation in Chriſt ; whether it be a possible
Proposition that God the Father hates the Son ; or whether
it was possible that Chriſt could have taken upon Him
the likeness of a Woman, or of the Devil, or of an Ass, or
of a Stone, or of a Gourd ; and then how that Gourd
should have Preach't, wrought Miracles, or been hung on
the Cross ; and, what Peter had Consecrated, if he had
adminiſtred the Sacrament at what time the Body of
Chriſt hung upon the Cross ; or whether at the same time
he might be said to be Man ; whether after the Resurrec-
tion there will be any eating and drinking, since we are
so much afraid of hunger and thirſt in this world. There

are infinite of these subtile Trifles, and others more subtile than these ; of Notions, Relations, Inſtants, Formalities, Quiddities, Ecceities, which no one can perceive
without a Lynceus his eyes, that could look through a
ſtone-wall, and discover those things through the thickeſt
darkness that never were.

Add to this those their other Determinations, and those
too so contrary to common Opinion that those Oracles of
the Stoicks, which they call Paradoxes, seem in comparison
of these but blockish and idle :—as, 'tis a lesser crime to
kill a thousand men than to set a ſtitch on a poor man's
shooe on the Sabbath-day ; and that a man should rather
chuse that the whole world with all Food and Raiment, as
they say, should perish, than tell a lye, though never
so inconsiderable. And these moſt subtile subtilties are
rendred yet more subtile by the several Methods of so
many Schoolmen, that one might sooner wind himself
out of a Labyrinth than the entanglements of the Realiſts,
Nominaliſts, Thomiſts, Albertiſts, Occamiſts, Scotiſts.
Nor have I nam'd all the several Sects, but onely some of
the chief ; in all which there is so much Doctrine and so
much difficultie, that I may well conceive the Apoſtles, had
they been to deal with these new kind of Divines, had
needed to have pray'd in aid of some other Spirit.

Paul knew what Faith was, and yet when he saith, "Faith is the Substance of things hop'd for, and the Evidence of things not seen", he did not define it Doctorlike. And as he understood Charity well himself, so he did as Illogically divide and define it to others in his first Epistle to the Corinthians, Chapter the thirteenth. And devoutly, no doubt, did the Apostles consecrate the Eucharist; yet, had they been askt the question touching the "Terminus a quo" and the "Terminus ad quem" of Transubstantiation; of the manner how the same body can be in several places at one and the same time; of the difference the body of Christ has in Heaven from that of the Cross, or this in the Sacrament; in what punct of time Transubstantiation is, whereas Prayer, by means of which it is, as being a discrete quantity, is transient; they would not, I conceive, have answer'd with the same subtilty as the Scotists Dispute and Define it.

They knew the Mother of Jesus; but which of them has so Philosophically demonstrated how she was preserv'd from Original sin, as have done our Divines? Peter receiv'd the Keyes, and from Him too that would not have trusted them with a person unworthy; yet whether he had understanding or no, I know not, for certainly he never attain'd to that subtilty to determine how he could

193

have the Key of knowledge that had no knowledge himself. They Baptized far and near, and yet taught no where
what was the Formal, Material, Efficient, and final cause
of Baptisme ; nor made the least mention of delible and
indelible Characters. They worshipt, 'tis true, but in Spirit,
following herein no other than that of the Gospel, " God
is a Spirit, and they that worship, must worship him in
Spirit and Truth "; yet it does not appear it was at that
time reveal'd to them that an Image sketcht on the Wall
with a Cole, was to be worshipt with the same worship as
Christ Himself, if at least the two 'fore fingers be stretcht
out, the hair long and uncut, and have three Rayes about
the Crown of the Head. For who can conceive these things,
unless he has spent at least six and thirty years in the Philosophical and Supercoelestial Whims of Aristotle and the
Schoolmen ?

In like manner, the Apostles press to us Grace ; but
which of them distinguisheth between free grace and
grace that makes a man acceptable ? They exhort us to
good works, and yet determine not what is the work
working, and what a resting in the work done. They in-
cite us to Charity, and yet make no difference between
Charity infus'd and Charity wrought in us by our own
endeavours. Nor do they declare whether it be an Acci-

dent or a Subſtance, a thing Created or Uncreated. They deteſt and abominate sin, but let me not live if they could define according to Art what that is which we call Sin, unless perhaps they were inspir'd by the spirit of the Scotiſts. Nor can I be brought to believe that Paul, by whose learning you may judge the reſt, would have so often condemn'd Queſtions, Disputes, Genealogies, and, as himself calls 'em, "Strifes of words", if he had thoroughly underſtood those subtilties ; especially when all the Debates and Controversies of those times were rude and blockish, in comparison of the more than Chrysip-pean subtilties of our Maſters.

Although yet the Gentlemen are so modeſt, that if they meet with any thing written by the Apoſtles not so smooth and even as might be expeſted from a Maſter, they do not presently condemn it, but handsomly bend it to their own purpose ; so great Respeſt and Honour do they give, partly to Antiquity and partly to the name of Apoſtle. And truly 'twere a kind of injuſtice to require so great things of them that never heard the leaſt word from their Maſters concerning it. And so if the like happen in Chrysoſtome, Basil, Jerome, they think it enough to say, They are not oblig'd by 't.

The Apoſtles also confuted the Heathen Philosophers

and Jews, a people than whom none more obstinate ; but rather by their good Lives and Miracles than Syllogisms : and yet there was scarce one amongst 'em that was capable of understanding the least " Quodlibet " of the Scotists. But now, where is that Heathen or Heretick that must not presently stoop to such Wire-drawn subtilties, unless he be so thick-skul'd that he can't apprehend 'em, or so impudent as to hiss 'em down, or, being furnisht with the same Tricks, be able to make his party good with 'em ? As if a man should set a Conjurer on work against a Conjurer, or fight with one hallowed Sword against another, which would prove no other than a work to no purpose. For my own part I conceive the Christians would do much better, if instead of those dull Troops and Companies of Souldiers, with which they have manag'd their War with such doubtful success, they would send the bauling Scotists, the most obstinate Occamists, and invincible Albertists to war against the Turks and Saracens ; and they would see, I guess a most pleasant Combate, and such a Victory as was never before. For who is so faint whom their devices will not enliven ? who so stupid whom such spurrs can't quicken ? or who so quick-sighted, before whose eyes they can't cast a mist ?

But you'l say, I jest. Nor are ye without cause, since

even amongſt Divines themselves there are some that have learnt better, and are ready to turn their ſtomachs at those foolish subtilties of t' others. There are some that deteſt 'em as a kind of Sacriledge, and count it the height of Impiety to speak so irreverently of such hidden things, rather to be ador'd than explicated ; to dispute of 'em with such profane and Heathenish niceties ; to define 'em so arrogantly, and pollute the majestie of Divinity with such pithless and sordid terms and opinions. Mean time the others please, nay hug themselves in their happiness, and are so taken up with these pleasant trifles, that they have not so much leisure as to caſt the leaſt eye on the Gospel or S. Paul's Epiſtles. And while they play the fool at this rate in their Schools, they make account the Universal Church would otherwise perish, unless, as the Poets fancy'd of Atlas that he supported Heaven with his shoulders, they underpropt t' other with their Syllogiſtical Buttresses.

And how great a happiness is this, think ye ? while, as if holy Writ were a Nose of Wax, they fashion and re-fashion it according to their pleasure ; while they require that their own Conclusions, subscrib'd by two or three Schoolmen, be accounted greater than Solon's Laws, and prefer'd before the Papal Decretals ; while, as Censors of the world, they force every one to a Recantation, that differs but a hair's bredth from the leaſt of their Explicit or Implicit Determinations. And those too they pronounce like Oracles. This Proposition is scandalous ; this Ir-reverent ; this has a smatch of Heresie ; this no very good sound : so that neither Baptisme, nor the Gospel, nor Paul, nor Peter, nor St. Jerome, nor St. Auguſtine, no nor moſt Ariſtotelitotical Thomas himself, can make a man a Chriſtian, without these Batchelours too be pleas'd to give him his grace. And the like is their subtilty in judging ; for who would think he were no Chriſtian that should say these two Speeches " Matula Putes " and " matula Putet ", or " Ollae fervere " and "ollam fervere " were not both good Latine, unless their wisdomes had taught us the contrary ? who had deliver'd the Church from such Miſts of Errour, which yet no one e'er met with, had they not come out with some University Seal for 't ? And are they not most happy while they do these things ?

Then for what concerns Hell, how exaſtly they describe every thing, as if they had been conversant in that Com-mon-wealth moſt part of their time ! Again, how do they frame in their fancy new Orbes, adding to those we have already an eighth ! a goodly one, no doubt, and spatious enough, leſt perhaps their happy Souls might lack room

*Then for what concerns Hell, how exactly do they
describe everything as if they had actually been there*

to walk in, entertain their friends, and now and then play at Foot-ball. And with these and a thousand the like fopperies their heads are so full ſtufft and ſtretcht, that I believe Jupiter's brain was not near so bigg when, being in labour with Pallas, he was beholding to the Mid-wifery of Vulcan's Axe. And therefore ye must not wonder if in their publique Disputes they are so bound about the head, leſt otherwise perhaps their brains might leap out.

Nay, I have sometimes laught my self, to see 'em so towre in their own opinion when they speak moſt bar-barously ; and when they Humh and Hawh so pitifully that none but one of their own Tribe can underſtand 'em, they call it heights which the Vulgar can't reach ; for they say 'tis beneath the dignity of Divine Myſteries to be crampt and ty'd up to the narrow Rules of Grammarians : from whence we may conjecture the great Prerogative of Divines, if they onely have the priviledge of speaking cor-ruptly, in which yet every Cobler thinks himself con-cern'd for his share. Laſtly, they look upon themselves as somewhat more than Men, as often as they are devoutly saluted by the name of " Our Maſters ", in which they fancy there lyes as much as in the Jews' " Jehovah "; and therefore they reckon it a crime if " Magiſter noſter " be written other than in Capital Letters ; and if any one should preposterously say "Noster magister", he has at once overturn'd the whole body of Divinity.

Monks That Call Themselves Religious

And next these come those that commonly call themselves the Religious and Monks ; most false in both Titles, when both a great part of 'em are farthest from Religion, and no men swarm thicker in all places than themselves. Nor can I think of any thing that could be more miserable, did not I support 'em so many several wayes. For whereas all men detest 'em to that height, that they take it for ill luck to meet one of 'em by chance, yet such is their happiness that they flatter themselves. For first, they reckon it one of the main Points of Piety if they are so illiterate that they can't so much as read. And then when they run over their Offices, which they carry about 'em, rather by tale than understanding, they believe the Gods more than ordinarily pleas'd with their braying. And some there are among 'em that put off their trumperies at vast rates, yet roave up and down for the bread they eat ; nay, there is scarce an Inne, Waggon, or Ship into which they intrude not, to the no small damage of the Common-wealth of Beggars. And yet, like pleasant fellows, with all this Vileness, Ignorance, Rudeness and Im-

Nay, there is scarce an inn, wagon or ship into which
they intrude not

pudence, they represent to us, for so they call it, the lives
of the Apoſtles.

Yet what is more pleasant than that they do all things
by Rule and, as it were, a kind of Mathematicks, the leaſt
swerving from which were a crime beyond forgiveness :—
as, how many knots their shooes must be ti'd with, or what
colour every thing is, what diſtinction of habits, of what
ſtuffe made, how many ſtraws broad their Girdles and
of what fashion, how many bushels wide their Cowle,
how many fingers long their Hair, and how many hours
sleep ; which exact equality, how disproportionable it is,
among such variety of bodies and tempers, who is there
that does not perceive it ? And yet by reason of these
fooleries they not onely set slight by others, but each
different Order, men otherwise professing Apoſtolical
Charity, despise one another, and for the different wearing
of a habit, or that 'tis of darker colour, they put all things
in combuſtion. And amongſt these there are some so
rigidly Religious that their upper Garment is hair-Cloth,
their inner of the fineſt Linnen ; and, on the contrary,
others wear Linnen without, and hair next their skins.
Others, agen, are as affraid to touch mony as poyson, and
yet neither forbear Wine nor dallying with Women. In
a word, 'tis their onely care that none of 'em come near

one another in their manner of living, nor do they endeavour how they may be like Chriſt, but how they may
differ among themselves.

And another great happiness they conceive in their
Names, while they call themselves Cordiliers, and among
these too, some are Colletes, some Minors, some Minims,
some Crossed ; and agen, these are Benedictines, those
Bernardines; these Carmelites, those Auguſtines ; these
Williamites, and those Jacobines ; as if it were not worth
the while to be call'd Chriſtians. And of these, a great
part build so much on their Ceremonies and petty Traditions of Men, that they think one Heaven is too poor a
reward for so great merit ; little dreaming that the time
will come when Chriſt, not regarding any of these trifles,
will call 'em to account for His precept of Charity.

One shall shew ye a large Trough full of all kinds of
Fish ; another tumble ye out so many bushels of Prayers ;
another reckon ye so many myriads of Faſts, and fetch
'em up agen in one dinner by eating till he cracks agen ;
another produces more bundles of Ceremonies than seven
of the ſtouteſt Ships would be able to carry ; another brags
he has not toucht a penny these three score Years without
two pair of Gloves at leaſt upon his hands ; another wears
a Cowl so lin'd with grease that the pooreſt Tarpaulin

Another will tell you he has lived these last fifty-five
years fastened to the same spot

would not ſtoop to take it up ; another will tell ye he has liv'd these fifty five Years like a Spunge, continually faſtned to the same place ; another is grown hoarse with his daily chanting ; another has contracted a Lethargy by his solitary living ; and another the Palsie in his Tongue for want of speaking.

But Chriſt, interrupting them in their vanities, which otherwise were endless, will ask 'em, " Whence this new kind of Jews ? I acknowledge one Commandment, which is truly mine, of which alone I hear nothing. I promiſt, 'tis true, my Father's heritage, and that without Parables, not to Cowls, odd Prayers, and Faſtings, but to the duties of Faith and Charity. Nor can I acknowledge them that leaſt acknowledge their faults. They that would seem holier than my self, let 'em if they liſt possess to themselves those three hundred sixty five Heavens of Basilides the Heretick's invention, or command them whose foolish Traditions they have prefer'd before my Preceps, to erect them a new one ". When they shall hear these things, and see common ordinary persons preferr'd before 'em, with what countenance, think ye, will they behold one another ? In the mean time they are happy in their hopes, and for this also they are beholding to me.

And yet these kind of people, though they are as it

were of another Common-wealth, no man dares despise ;
especially those begging Friars, because they are privie to
all men's secrets by means of Confessions, as they call 'em.
Which yet were no less than treason to discover, unless,
being got drunk, they have a mind to be pleasant, and
then all comes out, that is to say by hints and conjectures,
but suppressing the names. But if any one should anger
these Wasps, they'll sufficiently revenge themselves in
their publique Sermons, and so point out their enemy by
circumlocutions that there's no one but underſtands whom
'tis they mean, unless he underſtand nothing at all ; nor
will they give over their barking till you throw the Dogs
a bone.

And now tell me, what Jugler or Mountebank you had
rather behold than hear them rhetorically play the fool
in their Preachments, and yet moſt sweetly imitating
what Rhetoricians have written touching the Art of good
speaking ? Good God ! what several poſtures they have !
How they shift their voice, sing out their words, skip up
and down, and are ever and anon making such new faces,
that they confound all things with noise ! and yet this
Knack of theirs is no less than a Myſtery that runs in succession from one brother to another ; which though it be
not lawful for me to know, however I'll venture at it by

conjectures. And firſt they invoke what ever they have scrapt from the Poets; and in the next place, if they are to discourse of Charity, they take their rise from the river Nilus; or to set out the Myſtery of the Cross, from Bell and the Dragon; or to dispute of Faſting, from the twelve signs of the Zodiack; or, being to preach of Faith, ground their matter on the square of a Circle.

I have heard my self one, and he no small fool,—I was miſtaken, I would have said Scholar,—that being in a Famous Assembly explaining the Myſtery of the Trinity, that he might both let 'em see his Learning was not ordinary, and withal satisfie some Theological ears, he took a new way, to wit from the Letters, Syllables, and the Word it self; then from the Cohærence of the Nominative Case and the Verb, and the Adjeʧtive and Subſtantive: and while moſt of the Auditory wonder'd, and some of 'em mutter'd that of Horace, "what does all this Trumpery drive at?" at laſt he brought the matter to this head, that he would demonſtrate that the Myſtery of the Trinity was so clearly expreſt in the very Rudiments of Grammar, that the beſt Mathematician could not chalk 't out more plainly. And in this Discourse did this moſt Superlative Theologue beat his brains for eight whole moneths, that at this hour he's as blind as a Beetle, to wit, all the sight of his eyes being run into the sharpness of his wit. But for all that he nothing forthinketh his blindness, rather taking the same for too cheap a price of such a glory as he wan thereby.

And besides him I met with another, some eighty years of age, and such a Divine that you'd have sworn Scotus himself was reviv'd in him. He, being upon the point of unfolding the Mystery of the name Jesus, did with wonderful subtilty demonstrate that there lay hidden in those Letters what ever could be said of him ; for that it was only declin'd with three Cases, he said, it was a manifest token of the Divine Trinity ; and then, that the first ended in S, the second in M, the third in U, there was in it an ineffable Mystery, to wit, those three Letters declaring to us that he was the Beginning, Middle, and End of all. Nay, the Mystery was yet more abstruse ; for he so Mathematically split the word Jesus into two equal parts, that he left the middle letter by it self, and then told us that that letter in Hebrew was *Schin* or *Sin,* and that *Sin* in the Scotch tongue, as he remember'd, signifi'd as much as Sin ; from whence he gather'd that it was Jesus that took away the sins of the world. At which new Exposition the Auditory were so wonderfully intent and struck with admiration, especially the Theologues, that there

*Here they beat into the people's ears those magnifical
titles of illustrious doctors, subtile doctors, seraphic
doctors, cherubic doctors, and the like*

wanted little but that Niobe-like they had been turn'd to
Stones; whereas the like had almost happen'd to me, as
befell the Priapus in Horace.

And not without cause, for when were the Grecian
Demosthenes or Roman Cicero e'er guilty of the like?
They thought that Introduction faulty that was wide of
the Matter, as if it were not the way of Carters and Swin-
heards, that have no more wit than God sent 'em. But
these learned men think their Preamble, for so they call
it, then chiefly Rhetorical when it has least Coherence
with the rest of the Argument, that the admiring Auditory may in the mean while whisper to themselves, " What
will he be at now"? In the third place, they bring in
instead of Narration some Texts of Scripture, but handle
'em cursorily, and as it were by the bye, when yet it is
the onely thing they should have insisted on. And fourthly,
as it were changing a Part in the Play, they bolt out with
some question in Divinity, and many times relating
neither to Earth nor Heaven, and this they look upon as
a piece of Art.

Here they erect their Theological Crests, and beat into
the people's ears those Magnifical Titles of Illustrious
Doctors, Subtile Doctors, most Subtile Doctors, Seraphick
Doctors, Cherubin-Doctors, Holy Doctors, Unquestion-

able Doctors, and the like ; and then throw abroad among the ignorant people Syllogisms, Majors, Minors, Conclusions, Corollaries, Suppositions, and those so weak and foolish that they are below Pedantry. There remains yet the fifth Act, in which one would think they should shew their Mastery. And here they bring in some foolish insipid Fable out of *Speculum Historiale* or *Gesta Romanorum,* and Expound it Allegorically, Tropologically, and Anagogically. And after this manner do they end their Chimæra, and such as Horace despair'd of compassing, when he writ " Humano capiti," &c.

But they have heard from some body, I know not whom, that the beginning of a Speech should be Sober and Grave, and least given to noise. And therefore they begin theirs at that rate they can scarce hear themselves, as if it were no matter whether any one understood 'em. They have learnt some where that to move the affections a lowder voice is requisite. Whereupon they that otherwise would speak like a Mouse in a Cheese, start out of a suddain into a downright fury, even there too, where there's the least need of it. A man would swear they were past the power of Hellebor, so little do they consider where 'tis they run out.

Again, because they have heard that as a Speech comes

up to something, a man should press it more earnestly,
they, how ever they begin, use a strange contention of
voice in every part, though the Matter it self be never so
flat, and end in that manner as if they'd run themselves
out of breath. Lastly, they have learnt that among Rhetoricians there is some mention of Laughter, and therefore
they study to prick in a jest here and there ; but, O Venus !
so void of wit and so little to the purpose, that it may be
truly call'd an Asses playing on the Harp. And sometimes also they use somewhat of a sting, but so nevertheless that they rather tickle than wound ; nor do they ever
more truly flatter than when they would seem to use the
greatest freedom of speech.

Lastly, such is their whole action that a man would
swear they had learnt it from our common Tumblers,
though yet they come short of 'em in every respect. However, they are both so like, that no man will dispute but
that either these learnt their Rhetorick from them, or they
theirs from these. And yet they light on some that, when
they hear 'em, conceive they hear very Demosthenes and
Ciceroes : of which sort chiefly are our Merchants and
Women, whose Ears onely they endeavour to please, because as to the first, if they stroake 'em handsomely, some

part or other of their ill-gotten goods is wont to fall to
their share. And the Women, though for many other
things they favour this Order, this is not the least, that
they commit to their breasts what ever discontents they
have against their Husbands.

And now, I conceive me, ye see how much this kind of
people are beholding to me, that with their Petty Ceremonies, Ridiculous Trifles, and Noise, exercise a kind of
Tyranny among mankind, believing themselves very
Pauls and Anthonies.

Some Small Touches of Princes
and Courts

But I willingly give over these Stage-players, that are
such ingrateful dissemblers of the courtesies I have done
'em, and such impudent pretenders to Religion which
they ha' n't. And now I have a mind to give some small
touches of Princes and Courts, of whom I am had in
reverence, above-board and, as it becomes Gentlemen,
frankly. And truly, if they had the least proportion of
sound judgment, what life were more unpleasant than
theirs, or so much to be avoided ? For who ever did but
truly weigh with himself how great a burthen lies upon
his shoulders that would truly discharge the duty of a

*A prince who, like a fatal comet, is sent to bring
mischief and destruction*

Prince, he would not think it worth his while to make his way to a Crown by Perjury and Parricide.

He would consider that he that takes a Scepter in his hand should manage the Publick, not his Private Interest; study nothing but the common good; and not in the least go contrary to those Laws whereof himself is both the Author and Exactor: that he is to take an account of the good or evil administration of all his magistrates and subordinate Officers; that, though he is but one, all men's Eyes are upon him, and in his power it is, either like a good Planet to give life and safety to mankind by his harmless influence, or like a fatal Comet to send mischief and destruction: that the vices of other men are not alike felt, nor so generally communicated; and that a Prince stands in that place that his least deviation from the Rule of Honesty and Honour reaches farther than himself, and opens a gap to many men's ruine.

Besides, that the fortune of Princes has many things attending it that are but too apt to train 'em out of the way, as Pleasure, Liberty, Flattery, Excess; for which cause he should the more diligently endeavour and set a watch o'er himself, lest perhaps he be led aside and fail in his duty. Lastly, to say nothing of Treasons, ill will and such other Mischiefs he's in jeopardy of, that that True King is over his head, who in a short time will call him to account for every the least trespass, and that so much the more severely, by how much more mighty was the Empire committed to his charge. These and the like if a Prince should duly weigh, and weigh it he would if he were wise, he would neither be able to sleep nor take any hearty repast.

But now by my courtesie they leave all this care to the Gods, and are onely taken up with themselves, not admitting any one to their eare but such as know how to speak pleasant things, and not trouble 'em with business. They believe they have discharg'd all the duty of a Prince if they Hunt every day, keep a Stable of fine Horses, sell dignities and Commanderies, and invent new wayes of draining the Citizens' Purses and bringing it into their own Exchequer ; but under such dainty new-found names, that though the thing be most injust in it self, it carries yet some face of equity ; adding to this some little sweetnings, that what ever happens, they may be secure of the common people.

And now suppose some one, such as they sometimes are, a man ignorant of Laws, little less than an enemy to the publique good, and minding nothing but his own, given up to Pleasure, a hater of Learning, Liberty, and

Justice, studying nothing less than the publique safety, but measuring every thing by his own will and profit; and then put on him a golden Chain, that declares the accord of all Vertues linkt one to another; a Crown set with Diamonds, that should put him in mind how he ought to excell all others in Heroick Vertues; besides a Scepter, the Emblem of Justice and an untainted heart; and lastly, a Purple Robe, a Badge of that Charity he owes the Common-wealth. All which if a Prince should compare 'em with his own life, he would I believe be clearly asham'd of his bravery, and be afraid lest some or other gibing Expounder turn all this Tragical Furniture into a ridiculous Laughing-stock.

And as to the Court-Lords, what should I mention them? than most of whom though there be nothing more indebted, more servile, more witless, more contemptible, yet they would seem as they were the most excellent of all others. And yet in this only thing no men more modest, in that they are contented to wear about 'em Gold, Jewels, Purple, and those other marks of Vertue and Wisdome, but for the study of the things themselves, they remit it to others; thinking it happiness enough for them that they can call the King Master, have learnt the cringe *à la mode,* know when and where to use those Titles of

Your Grace, My Lord, Your Magnificence ; in a word
that they are paſt all shame and can flatter pleasantly.
For these are the Arts that speak a man truly Noble and
an exaɕt Courtier.

But if ye look into their manner of life you'll find 'em
meer Sots, as debaucht as Penelope's Wooers ; you know
the other part of the verse, which the Echo will better
tell ye than I can. They sleep till noon, and have their
mercenary Levite come to their bed side, where he chops
over his Mattins before they are half up. Then to Break-
faſt, which is scarce done but Dinner ſtaies for 'em. From
thence they go to Dice, Tables, Cards, or entertain themselves with Jeſters, Fools, Gambolls, and Horse-tricks.
In the mean time they have one or two Bevers, and then
Supper, and after that a Banquet, and 'twere well, by
Jupiter, there were no more than one.

And in this manner do their Hours, Dayes, Moneths,
Years, Age slide away without the leaſt irksomeness. Nay,
I have sometimes gone away many Inches fatter, to see
'em speak bigg words ; whiles each of the Ladies believes
her self so much nearer to the Gods, by how much the
longer train she trails after her ; whiles one Nobleman
edges out another, that he may get the nearer to Jupiter
himself ; and every one of 'em pleases himself the more

They put on him a crown set with diamonds, besides a scepter and a purple robe

by how massier is the Chain he swaggs on his shoulders, as if he meant to shew his ſtrength as well as his wealth.

The Lights of the World Reduced to a mere Wallet

Nor are Princes by themselves in their manner of life, since Popes, Cardinals, and Bishops have so diligently follow'd their ſteps, that they've almoſt got the ſtart of 'em. For if any of 'em would consider what their Albe should put 'em in mind of, to wit a blameless life ; what is meant by their forked Miters, whose each point is held in by the same knot, wee'll suppose it a perfeᵃ knowledge of the Old and New Teſtaments ; what those Gloves on their Hands, but a sincere adminiſtration of the Sacraments, and free from all touch of worldly business ; what their Crosier, but a careful looking after the Flock committed to their charge ; what the Cross born before 'em, but viᵃory over all earthly affeᵃions :—these, I say, and many of the like kind should any one truly consider, would he not live a sad and troublesome life ?

Whereas now they do well enough while they feed themselves onely ; and for the care of their Flock, either put it over to Chriſt or lay it all on their Suffragans, as they call 'em, or some poor Vicars. Nor do they so much

as remember their name, or what the word Bishop signi-
fies ; to wit, Labour, Care and Trouble. But in racking
to gather moneys they truly act the part of Bishops, and
herein acquit themselves to be no blind Seers.

In like manner Cardinals, if they thought themselves the
successours of the Apostles, they would likewise imagine
that the same things the other did are requir'd of them,
and that they are not Lords, but Dispensers of Spiritual
things, of which they must shortly give an exact account.
But if they also would a little Philosophize on their Habit,
and think with themselves what's the meaning of their
Linen Rochet ; is it not a remarkable and singular integrity of life ? what that inner Purple ; is it not an
earnest and fervent love of God ? or what that outward,
whose loose Plaits and long Train fall round his Reverence's Mule, and are large enough to cover a Camel ;
is it not Charity, that spreads it self so wide to the succour of all men ? that is, to Instruct, Exort, Comfort,
Reprehend, Admonish, compose Wars, resist wicked
Princes, and willingly expend, not onely their Wealth
but their very Lives for the Flock of Christ : though yet
what need at all of wealth to them that supply the room
of the poor Apostles ?—These things, I say, did they but
duely consider, they would not be so ambitious of that

216

Dignity ; or, if they were, they would willingly leave it
and live a laborious, careful life, such as was that of the
antient Apostles.

And for Popes, that supply the place of Christ, if they
should endeavour to imitate His Life, to wit His Poverty,
Labour, Doctrine, Cross, and contempt of Life, or should
they consider what the name Pope, that is Father, or Holiness, imports, who would live more disconsolate than
themselves ? or who would purchase that Chair with all
his substance ? or defend it so purchast, with Swords,
Poisons, and all force imaginable ? so great a profit would
the access of Wisdom deprive him of ;—Wisdom did I
say ? nay, the least corn of that Salt which Christ speaks
of : so much Wealth, so much Honour, so much Riches,
so many Victories, so many Offices, so many Dispensa-
tions, so much Tribute, so many Pardons ; such Horses,
such Mules, such Guards, and so much Pleasure would it
lose them.

You see how much I have comprehended in a little :
instead of which it would bring in Watchings, Fastings,
Tears, Prayers, Sermons, good Endeavours, Sighs, and
a thousand the like troublesome Exercises. Nor is this least
considerable : so many Scribes, so many Copying Clerks,
so many Notaries, so many Advocates, so many Pro-

217

mooters, so many Secretaries, so many Muletters, so many
Grooms, so many Bankers : in short, that vaſt multitude
of men that overcharge the Roman See—I miſtook, I
meant honour—, might beg their bread.

A moſt inhumane and abominable thing, and more to
be execrated, that those great Princes of the Church and
true Lights of the World should be reduc'd to a Staff and
a Wallet. Whereas now, if there be any thing that re-
quires their pains, they leave that to Peter and Paul that
have leisure enough ; but if there be any thing of Honour
or Pleasure, they take that to themselves. By which means
it is, yet by my courtesie, that scarce any kind of men
live more voluptuously or with less trouble ; as believing
that Chriſt will be well enough pleas'd, if in their Myſtical
and almoſt mimical Pontificalibus, Ceremonies, Titles
of Holiness and the like, and Blessing and Cursing, they
play the parts of Bishops. To work Miracles is old and
antiquated, and not in fashion now ; to inſtruct the people, troublesome ; to interpret the Scripture, Pedantick ;
to pray, a sign one has little else to do ; to shed tears, silly
and womanish ; to be poor, base ; to be vanquisht, dis-
honourable, and little becoming him that scarce admits
even Kings to kiss his Slipper ; and laſtly, to dye, un-
couth ; and to be ſtretcht on a Cross, infamous.

So many scribes, so many copying clerks, so many notaries, advocates and secretaries

Theirs are only those Weapons and sweet Blessings which Paul mentions, and of these truly they are bountiful enough : as Interdictions, Hangings, Heavy Burthens, Reproofs, Anathemas, Executions in Effigie, and that terrible Thunder-bolt of Excommunication, with the very sight of which they sink men's Souls beneath the bottom of Hell : which yet these most holy Fathers in Christ and his Vicars hurl with more fierceness against none than against such as, by the instigation of the Devil, attempt to lessen or rob 'em of Peter's Patrimony. When, though these words in the Gospel, " We have left all, and follow'd Thee," were his, yet they call his Patrimony Lands, Cities, Tribute, imposts, Riches ; for which, being enflam'd with the love of Christ, they contend with Fire and Sword, and not without losse of much Christian blood, and believe they have then most Apostolically defended the Church, the Spouse of Christ, when the enemy, as they call 'em, are valiantly routed. As if the Church had any deadlier enemies than wicked Prelates, who not onely suffer Christ to run out of request for want of preaching him, but hinder his spreading by their multitudes of Laws, meerly contriv'd for their own profit, corrupt him by their forc'd Expositions, and murder him by the evil example of their pestilent life.

Nay, further, whereas the Church of Christ was founded in blood, confirm'd by blood, and augmented by blood, now, as if Christ, who after his wonted manner defends his people, were lost, they govern all by the Sword. And whereas War is so Savage a thing that it rather befits Beasts than Men, so outragious that the very Poets feign'd it came from the Furies, so pestilent that it corrupts all men's manners, so injust that it is best executed by the worst of men, so wicked that it has no agreement with Christ; and yet, omitting all the other, they make this their onely business.

Here you'll see decrepit old fellows acting the parts of young men, neither troubled at their costs nor weari'd with their labours, nor discourag'd at any thing, so they may have the liberty of turning Laws, Religion, Peace and all things else quite topsie turvie. Nor are they destitute of their learned Flatterers that call that palpable Madness Zeal, Piety, and Valour, having found out a new way by which a man may kill his brother without the least breach of that Charity which, by the command of Christ, one Christian owes another.

And here, in troth, I'm a little at a stand whether the Ecclesiastical German Electors gave 'em this example, or rather took it from 'em; who, laying aside their Habit,

War is so savage a thing

Benedictions and all the like Ceremonies, so act the part
of Commanders that they think it a mean thing, and least
beseeming a Bishop, to shew the least courage to God-
ward unless it be in a battle.

And as to the common Heard of Priests, they account
it a crime to degenerate from the Sanctity of their Prelates.
Heidah! how Souldier-like they bussle about the *jus
divinum* of Titles, and how quick-sighted they are to
pick the least thing out of the Writings of the Antients,
wherewith they may fright the common people, and convince 'em, if possible, that more than a Tenth is due!
Yet in the mean-time it least comes in their heads how
many things are every where extant concerning that duty
which they owe the people. Nor does their shorn Crown
in the least admonish 'em that a Priest should be free from
all worldly desires, and think of nothing but heavenly
things. Whereas on the contrary, these jolly fellows say
they have sufficiently discharg'd their Office if they but
any-how mumble over a few odd Prayers, which, so help
me, Hercules! I wonder if any God either hear or understand, since they do neither themselves; especially when
they thunder 'em out in that manner they are wont.

But this they have in common with those of the
Heathens, that they are vigilant enough to the harvest

of their profit, nor is there any of 'em that is not better read in those Laws than the Scripture. Whereas if there be any thing burthensome, they prudently lay that on other men's shoulders, and shift it from one to t'other, as men toss a Ball from hand to hand; following herein the example of Lay Princes, who commit the Government of their Kingdoms to their Grand Ministers, and they again to others, and leave all study of Piety to the common people. In like manner the common people put it over to those they call Ecclesiasticks, as if themselves were no part of the Church, or that their vow in Baptism had lost its obligation.

Again, the Priests that call themselves Secular, as if they were initiated to the world, not to Christ, lay the burthen on the Regulars; the Regulars on the Monks; the Monks that have more liberty, on those that have less; and all of 'em on the Mendicants; the Mendicants on the Carthusians, amongst whom, if any where, this Piety lies buried, but yet so close that scarce any one can perceive it. In like manner the Popes, the most diligent of all others in gathering in the Harvest of mony, refer all their Apostolical work to the Bishops; the Bishops to the Parsons; the Parsons to the Vicars; the Vicars to their brother

His net caught a great many fish though he himself was fast asleep

Mendicants; and they again throw back the care of the Flock on those that take the Wooll.

But it is not my business to sift too narrowly the lives of Prelates and Priests, for fear I seem to have intended rather a Satyr than an Oration, and be thought to tax good Princes while I praise the bad. And therefore, what I slightly taught before, has been to no other end but that it might appear that there's no man can live pleasant unless he be initiated to my Rites, and have me propitious to him.

Fortune Loves Those that Have the Least Wit

For how can it be otherwise, when Fortune, the great Directress of all Humane Affairs, and my self are so all one that she was always an enemy to those wise men, and on the contrary so favourable to Fools and careless fellows, that all things hit luckly to 'em?

You have heard of that Timotheus, the most fortunate General of the Athenians, of whom came that Proverb, " His Net caught fish, though he were asleep "; and that, " The Owl flies "; whereas these other hit properly, Wise men " born in the fourth moneth "; and again, " He rides Sejanus's his horse "; and "gold of Tolouse ", signifying

thereby the extremity of ill fortune. But I forbear the
further threading of Proverbs, leſt I seem to have pilfer'd
my friend Erasmus's Adagies. Fortune loves those that
have leaſt wit and moſt confidence, and such as like that
saying of Caesar, "The Dye is thrown". But Wisdome
makes men bashful, which is the reason that those Wise
men have so little to do, unless it be with Poverty, Hunger,
and Chimny-corners ; that they live such neglected, unknown and hated lives : whereas Fools abound in money,
have the chief Commands in the Common-wealth, and in
a word, flourish every way. For if it be a happiness to
please Princes, and to be conversant among those Golden
and Diamond Gods, what is more unprofitable than Wisdom, or what is it these kind of men have, may more
juſtly be censur'd ?

If Wealth is to be got, how little good at it is that Merchant like to do, if following the Precepts of Wisdom he
should boggle at Perjury ; or being taken in a lie, blush ;
or in the leaſt regard the sad scruples of those Wise-men
touching Rapine and Usury. Again, if a man sue for
Honours or Church-Preferments, an Ass or wild Oxe
shall sooner get 'em than a Wise man. If a man's in love
with a young Wench, none of the leaſt Humours in this
Comedy, they are wholly addicted to Fools, and are afraid

of a Wise man, and flie him as they would a Scorpion.
Laſtly, whoever intend to live merry and frolique, shut
their doors againſt Wise men, and admit any thing sooner.
In brief, go whither ye will, among Prelates, Princes,
Judges, Magiſtrates, Friends, Enemies, from higheſt to
loweſt, and you'll find all things done by money ; which,
as a Wise man contemns it, so it takes a special care not
to come near him.

Great Authors have made Folly Famous

What shall I say ? There is no measure or end of my
praises, and yet 'tis fit my Oration have an end. And therefore I'll ev'n break off ; and yet, before I do it, 'twill not
be amiss if I briefly shew ye that there has not been wanting even great Authours that have made me famous, both
by their Writings and Aĉtions, leſt perhaps otherwise I
may seem to have foolishly pleas'd my self only, or that
the Lawyers charge me that I have prov'd nothing. After
their example, therefore, will I alleadge my proofs, that
is to say, nothing to the point.

And firſt, every man allows this Proverb, " That where
a man wants matter, he may beſt frame some ". And to
this purpose is that Verse which we teach Children, " 'Tis
the greateſt wisdome to know when and where to coun-

terfeit the Fool". And now judge your selves what an
excellent thing this Folly is, whose very counterfeit and
semblance only has got such praise from the Learned.
But more candidly does that fat plump " Epicurean bacon-
hogg ", Horace, for so he calls himself, bid us " mingle
our purposes with Folly " ; and whereas he adds the
word *brevem,* short, perhaps to help out the Verse, he
might as well have let it alone ; and agen, " 'tis a pleasant
thing to play the fool in the right season " ; and in another
place, he had rather " be accounted a dottrel and sot, than
to be wise and made mouths at ". And Telemachus in
Homer, whom the Poet praises so much, is now and then
called νήπιος, Fool : and by the same name, as if there were
some good fortune in 't, are the Tragedians wont to call
Boyes and Striplings. And what does that sacred book of
Iliads contain, but a kind of counter-scuffle between foolish
Kings and foolish People ? Besides, how absolute is that
praise that Cicero gives of it ! " All things are full of
fools ". For who does not know that every good, the more
diffusive it is, by so much the better it is ?

But perhaps their authority may be of small credit
among Christians. Wee'l therefore, if you please, support
our praises with some Testimonies of holy Writ also ;
in the first place, neverthelesse, having forespoke our

226

Theologues that they'll give us leave to do it without offence. And in the next, forasmuch as we attempt a matter of some difficulty, and it may be perhaps a little too sawcy to call back agen the Muses from Helicon to so great a journey, especially in a matter they are wholly Strangers to; it will be more sutable, perhaps, while I play the Divine and make my way through such prickly quiddities, that I entreat the Soul of Scotus, a thing more briStlely than either Porcupine or Hedg-hog, to leave his Scorbone a while and come into my breSt, and then let him go whither he pleases, or to the dogs.

I could wish also that I might change my countenance, or that I had on the square Cap and the Cassock, for fear some or other should impeach me of theft, as if I had privily rifled our MaSters' Desks, in that I have got so much Divinity. But it ought not to seem so Strange, if after so long and intimate an acquaintance and converse with 'em, I have pickt up somewhat; when as that Fig-tree-god Priapus, hearing his owner read certain Greek words, took so much notice of 'em, that he got 'em by heart; and that Cock in Lucian, by having liv'd long amongSt men, became at laSt a maSter of their Language.

But to the point under a fortunate direction. EcclesiaStes saith in his firSt Chapter. "The number of fools is in-

finite " ; and when he calls it infinite, does he not seem to
comprehend all men, unless it be some few, whom yet
'tis a question whether any man ever saw ? But more
ingenuously does Jeremiah in his tenth Chapter confess
it, saying, " Every man is made a fool through his own
wisdome " ; attributing wisedom to God alone, and leaving folly to all men else : and agen, " Let not man glory in
his wisdome ". And why, good Jeremiah, would'st thou
not have a man glory in his wisedom ? Because, he'll say,
he has none at all.

But to return to Ecclesiastes, who, when he cries out,
" Vanity of Vanities, all is vanity ! " what other thoughts
had he, do ye believe, than that, as I said before, the life
of man is nothing else but an enterlude of Folly ? In which
he has added one voice more to that justly receiv'd praise
of Cicero's, which I quoted before, viz. " All things are
full of fools ". Agen, that wise Preacher that said, " A
fool changes as the Moon, but a wise man is permanent
as the Sun ", what else did he hint at in it, but that all
mankind are fools, and the name of Wise onely proper
to God ? For by the Moon Interpreters understand humane Nature, and by the Sun, God, the only Fountain
of light ; with which agrees that which Christ himself
in the Gospel denies, that any one is to be call'd good

The number of fools is infinite

but one, and that is God. And then if he is a fool that is not wise, and every good man according to the Stoicks is a wise man, it is no wonder if all mankind be concluded under Folly.

Again Solomon, Chap. 15, "Foolishnesse" saith he, " is joy to the Fool", thereby plainly confessing that without folly there is no pleasure in life. To which is pertinent that other, " He that encreaseth knowledge, encreaseth grief ; and in much understanding there is much indignation ". And does he not plainly confess as much, Chap. 7, " The heart of the wise is where sadness is, but the heart of fools follows mirth " ? by which you see, he thought it not enough to have learnt wisedome, without he had added the knowledge of me also.

And if ye will not believe me, take his own words, Chap. 1, " I gave my heart to know wisdome and knowledge, madnesse and folly ". Where, by the way, 'tis worth your remark, that he intended me somewhat extraordinary, that he nam'd me last. A Preacher writ it, and this you know is the order among Church-men, that he that is first in Dignity comes last in place, as mindful no doubt, what ever they do in other things, herein at least to observe the Evangelical precept.

Besides, that Folly is more excellent than Wisdom, the

Son of Sirach, who ever he were, clearly witnesseth, Chap. 44, whose words, so help me Hercules ! I shall not once utter before you meet my Induction with a sutable answer, according to the manner of those in Plato that dispute with Socrates. What things are more proper to be laid up with care, such as are rare and precious, or such as are common and of no account ? Why do you give me no answer ? Well, though ye should dissemble, the Greek Proverb will answer for ye, "Fowl Water is thrown out of doors " ; which, if any man shall be so ungratious as to contemn, let him know 'tis Aristotle's, the god of our Masters'. Is there any of ye so very a Fool as to leave Jewels and Gold in the street ? In troth, I think not ; in the most secret part of your Houses ; nor is that enough, if there be any Drawer in your Iron Chests more private than other, there ye lay 'em ; but dirt ye throw out of doors. And therefore, if ye so carefully lay up such things as you value, and throw away what's vile and of no worth, is it not plain that Wisdom, which he forbids a man to hide, is of less account than Folly, which he commands him to cover ? Take his own words, " Better is the man that hideth his Folly than he that hideth his Wisdom ".

Or what is that, when he attributes an upright mind without Craft or Malice to a Fool, when a wise man the

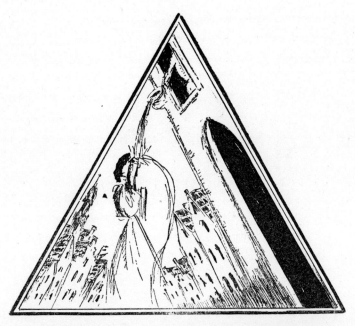

Foul water is thrown out of doors, sayeth Aristotle

while thinks no man like himself? For so I understand
that in his Tenth Chap., "A Fool walking by the way,
being a fool himself, supposes all men to be fools like
him". And is it not a signe of great integrity to
esteem every man as good as himself, and when there
is no one that leans not too much to 'ther way, to be so
frank yet as to divide his praises with another? Nor was
this great King asham'd of the Name, when he says of
himself that he is more foolish than any man. Nor did
Paul, that great Doctor of the Gentiles, writing to the
Corinthians, unwillingly acknowledg it; "I speak" saith
he, "like a fool. I am more". As if it could be any dishonour to excel in Folly.

Folly's Friend Erasmus

But here I meet with a great noise of some that endeavour to peck out the Crows' eyes; that is, to blind
the Doctors of our times, and smoak out their eyes with
new Annotations; among whom my friend Erasmus,
whom for honour's sake I often mention, deserves, if not
the first place, yet certainly the second. O most foolish
instance, they cry, and well becoming Folly her self! The
Apostle's meaning was wide enough from what thou
dream'st; for he spake it not in this sense, that he would

have them believe him a greater fool than the rest : but when he had said, "They are Ministers of Christ, the same am I", and by way of boasting herein, had equal'd himself with to 'thers, he added this by way of correction or checking himself, "I am more"; as meaning that he was not onely equal to the rest of the Apostles in the work of the Gospel, but somewhat superiour. And therefore, while he would have this receiv'd as a Truth, lest nevertheless it might not relish their eares as being spoken with too much Arrogance, he foreshorten'd his Argument with the Vizard of Folly, "I speak like a fool"; because he knew it was the Prerogative of fools to speak what they list, and that too without offence.

Whatever he thought when he writ this, I leave it to them to discuss; for my own part, I follow those fat, fleshie, and vulgarly approv'd Doctours, with whom by Jupiter ! a great part of the learned had rather err than follow them that understand the Tongues, though they are never so much in the right. Not any of 'em make greater account of those smatterers at Greek than if they were Dawes. Especially when a no small Professor, whose name I wittingly conceal, lest those Choughs should chatter at me that Greek Proverb I have so often mentioned, "an Asse at a Harp", discoursing Magisterially and

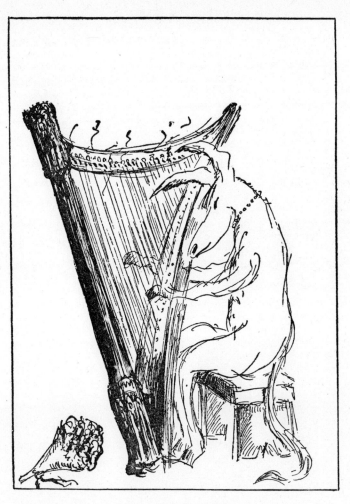

An ass playing the harp

Theologically on this Text, " I speak as a fool, I am more ",
drew a new Thesis ; and, which without the height of
Logick he could never have done, made this new Sub-
division—For I'll give ye his own words, not onely in form
but matter also—, " I speak like a fool " : that is, if you
look upon me as a fool for comparing my self with those
false Apostles, I shall seem yet a greater fool by esteeming
my self before 'em ; though the same person a little after,
as forgetting himself, runs off to another matter.

But why do I thus staggeringly defend my self with
one single instance ? As if it were not the common privi-
ledg of Divines to stretch Heaven, that is Holy Writ, like
a Cheverel ; and when there are many things in St. Paul
that thwart themselves, which yet in their proper place
do well enough, if there be any credit to be given to St.
Jerom, that was Master of five Tongues. Such was that
of his at Athens, when having casually espi'd the inscrip-
tion of that Altar, he wrested it into an Argument to
prove the Christian Faith, and leaving out all the other
words because they made against him, took notice onely
of the two last, viz. " To the unknown God " ; and those
too, not without some alteration, for the whole Inscrip-
tion was thus : " To the Gods of Asia, Europe, and
Africa ; To the unknown and strange Gods ". And ac-

cording to his example do the Sons of the Prophets, who, forcing out here and there four or five Expressions and if need be corrupting the sense, wreſt it to their own purpose ; though what goes before and follows after, make nothing to the matter in hand, nay, be quite againſt it. Which yet they do with so happy an impudence, that oftentimes the Civilians envie them that faculty.

For what is it in a manner they may not hope for success in, when this great Doctor (I had almoſt bolted out his name, but that I once agen ſtand in fear of the Greek Proverb) has made a conſtruction on an expression of Luke, so agreeable to the mind of Chriſt as are Fire and Water to one another. For when the laſt point of danger was at hand, at which time retainers and dependants are wont in a more special manner to attend their Protectours, to examine what ſtrength they have, and prepare for the encounter ; Chriſt, intending to take out of his Disciples' minds all truſt and confidence in such like defence, demands of them whether they wanted any thing, when he sent them forth so unprovided for a journey, that they had neither shoes to defend their feet from the injuries of ſtones and briers, nor the provision of a scrip to preserve 'em from hunger. And when they had denied that they wanted any thing, he adds, " But now, he that hath a bagg, let him take it, and likewise a scrip ; and he that hath none, let him sell his coat and buy a sword ".

And now when the summe of all that Christ taught prest onely Meekness, Suffering and Contempt of life, who does not clearly perceive what he means in this place ? to wit, that he might the more disarm his Ministers, that neglecting not onely Shoos and Scrip but throwing away their very Coat, they might, being in a manner naked, the more readily and with less hindrance take in hand the work of the Gospel, and provide themselves of nothing but a sword : not such as Thieves and Murtherers go up and down with, but the Sword of the Spirit, that pierceth the most inward parts, and so cuts off as it were at one blow, all earthly affections, that they mind nothing but their duty to God.

But see, I pray, whither this famous Theologue wrests it. By the Sword he interprets defence against persecution ; and by the Bagg sufficient provision to carry it on. As if Christ having alter'd his mind, in that he sent out his Disciples not so royally attended as he should have done, repented himself of his former instructions : or as forgetting that he had said, " Blessed are ye when ye are evil spoken of, despised, and persecuted, &c.", and forbad 'em to resist evil ; for that the meek in Spirit, not the proud, are blessed : or, left remembring, I say, that he had compar'd them to Sparrows and Lillies, thereby minding them what small care they should take for the things of this life, was so far now from having them go forth without a Sword, that he commanded 'em to get one, though with the sale of their Coat, and had rather they should go naked than want a brawling-iron by their sides. And to this, as under the word " Sword ", he conceives to be comprehended whatever appertains to the repelling of injuries ; so under that of " Scrip " he takes in whatever is necessary to the support of life.

And so does this deep Interpreter of the divine meaning bring forth the Apostles to preach the Doctrine of a crucified Christ, but furnisht at all points with Launces, Slings, Quarter-staffs, and Bombards ; lading 'em also with bag and baggage, left perhaps it might not be lawful for 'em to leave their Inn unlesse they were empty and fasting. Nor does he take the least notice of this, that he that so will'd the Sword to be bought, reprehends it a little after and commands it to be sheath'd ; and that it was never heard that the Apostles ever us'd or swords or bucklers against the Gentiles, though 'tis likely they had don 't, if Christ had ever intended, as this Doctor interprets.

What authority there was in Holy Writ that commands heretics to be convinced by fire rather than reclaimed by argument

Folly Attends a Theological Dispute

There is another, too, whose name out of respect I
pass by, a man of no small repute, who from those Tents
which Habbakkuk mentions, "The Tents of the land
of Midian shall tremble", drew this Exposition, that it
was prophesied of the skin of Saint Bartholomew, who
was flay'd alive. And why, forsooth, but because those
Tents were cover'd with skins ?

I was lately my self at a Theological dispute, for I am
often there, where when one was demanding, What authority there was in holy Writ that commands Hereticks
to be convinc'd by Fire rather than reclaim'd by Argument, a crabbed old fellow, and one whose supercilious
gravity spake him at least a Doctor, answered in a great
fume that Saint Paul had decreed it, who said, "Reject
him that is a Heretick, after once or twice admonition".
And when he had sundry times, one after another, thun-
dred out the same thing, and most men wondred what
ailed the man, at last he explain'd it thus, making two
words of one : "A Heretick must be put to death". Some
laught, and yet there wanted not others to whom this
Exposition seem'd plainly Theological ; which, when
some, though those very few, oppos'd, they cut off the

dispute, as we say, with a Hatchet, and the credit of so uncontroulable an Author. " Pray conceive me ", said he ; " it is written, ' Thou shalt not suffer a witch to live '. But every Heretick bewitches the people ; therefore, &c."

And now, as many as were present admir'd the man's wit, and consequently submitted to his decision of the Question. Nor came it into any of their heads that that Law concern'd onely Fortune-tellers, Enchanters, and Magicians, whom the Hebrews call in their Tongue " Mecaschephim ", Witches or Sorcerers : for otherwise, perhaps, by the same reason it might as well have extended to fornication and drunkenness.

But I foolishly run on in these matters, though yet there are so many of 'em that neither Chrysippus' nor Didymus's Volums are large enough to contain 'em. I would onely desire ye to consider this, that if so great Doctors may be allow'd this liberty, you may the more reasonably pardon even me also, a raw, effeminate Divine, if I quote not every thing so exactly as I should. And so at last I return to Paul. " Ye willingly ", saith he, " suffer my foolishness " ; and again, " Take me as a fool " ; and further, " I speak it not after the Lord, but as it were foolishly " ; and in another place, " We are fools for Christ's sake ".

Folly quotes Christ in her Praise

You have heard from how great an Author how great praises of Folly ; and to what other end, but that without doubt he look'd upon 't as that one thing both necessary and profitable. " If any one amongst ye ", saith he, " seem to be wise, let him be a fool, that he may be wise ". And in Luke, Jesus cal'd those two Disciples, with whom he joyn'd himself upon the way, "fools". Nor can I give ye any reason why it should seem so strange, when Saint Paul imputes a kind of folly even to God himself. " The foolishness of God", saith he, "is wiser than men ". Though yet I must confess that Origen upon the place denies that this foolishness may be resembled to the uncertain judgment of men ; of which kind is, that " the preaching of the cross is to them that perish foolishness ".

But why am I so careful to no purpose, that I thus run on to prove my matter by so many testimonies ? when in those mystical Psalms, Christ speaking to the Father sayes openly, " Thou knowest my foolishnesse". Nor is it without ground that fools are so acceptable to God. The reason perhaps may be this, that as Princes carry a suspicious eye upon those that are over-wise, and consequently hate 'em—as Caesar did Brutus and Cassius, when

he fear'd not in the least drunken Antony; so Nero,
Seneca; and Dionysius, Plato—, and on the contrary are
delighted in those blunter and unlabour'd wits; in like
manner Christ ever abhors and condemns those wise men,
and such as put confidence in their own wisdome. And
this Paul makes clearly out when he said, "God hath
chosen the foolish things of this world"; and when he
saith, "It pleased God by foolishness to save the world",
as well knowing it had been impossible to have reform'd
it by wisdom. Which also he sufficiently declares himself, crying out by the mouth of his Prophet, "I will
destroy the wisedom of the wise, and cast away the understanding of the prudent".

And agen, when Christ gives Him thanks that he had
conceal'd the Mystery of Salvation from the wise, but revealed it to babes and sucklings, that is to say, Fools. For
the Greek word for Babes is Fools, which he opposeth to
the word Wise men. To this appertains that throughout
the Gospel you find him ever accusing the Scribes and
Pharisees and Doctors of the Law, but diligently defending the ignorant multitude (for what other is that
"Woe to ye Scribes and Pharises", than woe to ye, ye
wise men?), but seems chiefly delighted in little Children, Women, and Fishers. Besides, among brute Beasts

You find him ever accusing the scribes, pharisees and doctors of law

he is best pleas'd with those that have least in 'em of the
Foxes subtilty. And therefore he chose rather to ride
upon an Asse, when, if he had pleas'd, he might have
bestrid the Lion without danger. And the Holy Ghost
came down in the shape of a Dove, not of an Eagle or
Kite.

Add to this that in Scripture there is frequent mention
of Harts, Hinds and Lambs ; and such as are destin'd
to eternal life are called sheep, than which creature there
is not any thing more foolish ; if we may believe that
Proverb of Aristotle " sheepish manners ", which he tells
us is taken from the foolishness of that creature, and is
us'd to be apply'd to dull-headed people and lack-wits.
And yet Christ professes to be the Shepheard of this Flock,
and is himself delighted with the name of a Lamb ; according to Saint John, " Behold the Lamb of God ! " Of
which also there is much mention in the Revelation. And
what does all this drive at, but that all mankind are fools
—nay, even the very best ?

And Christ himself, that he might the better relieve
this Folly, being the wisdome of the Father, yet in some
manner became a fool, when taking upon him the nature
of man, he was found in shape as a man ; as in like manner he was made Sin, that he might heal sinners. Nor did

241

he work this Cure any other way than by the foolishness
of the Cross, and a company of fat Apoſtles, not much
better, to whom also he carefully recommended folly, but
gave 'em a caution againſt wisdome, and drew 'em together by the Example of little Children, Lillies, Muſtard-
seed and Sparrows, things senseless and inconsiderable,
living only by the dictates of Nature and without either
craft or care. Besides, when he forbad 'em to be troubled
about what they should say before Governors, and
ſtraightly charg'd 'em not to enquire after times and sea-
sons, to wit, that they might not truſt to their own wisedom but wholly depend on him.

And to the same purpose is it that that great Architect
of the World, God, gave man an Injunction againſt his
eating of the Tree of Knowledge, as if knowledge were
the bane of happinesse ; according to which also, St. Paul
dis-allows it as puffing up and deſtructive ; whence also
St. Bernard seems in my opinion to follow, when he interprets that mountain whereon Lucifer had fixt his habitation, to be the mountain of knowledge.

Nor perhaps ought I to omit this other argument, that
folly is so gracious above, that her errors are only par-
doned, those of wise men never. Whence it is that they that
ask forgiveness, though they offend never so wittingly,

cloak it yet with the excuse of folly. So Aaron, in Numbers, if I mistake not the book, when he sues unto Moses concerning his Sister's leprosie, " I beseech thee, my Lord, not to lay this sin upon us, which we have foolishly committed ". So Saul makes his excuse to David, " For behold ", saith he, " I did it foolishly ". And again, David himself thus sweetens God, " And therefore I beseech thee, O Lord, to take away the trespass of thy Servant, for I have done foolishly " ; as if he knew there was no pardon to be obtain'd unlesse he had colour'd his offence with folly and ignorance.

And stronger is that of Christ upon the Cross when he pray'd for his enemies, " Father forgive them " ; nor does he cover their crime with any other excuse than that of unwittingnesse—because, saith he, " they know not what they do ". In like manner Paul, writing to Timothy, " But therefore I obtain'd mercy, for that I did it ignorantly through unbelief ". And what is the meaning of " I did it ignorantly " but that I did it out of folly, not malice ? And what of, " Therefore I receiv'd mercy ", but that I had not obtain'd it, had I not been made more allowable through the covert of folly ? For us also makes that mystical Psalmist, though I remembred it not in its right place, " Remember not the sins of my youth nor my ignorances ". You see what two things he pretends, to wit, Youth, whose companion I ever am, and Ignorances, and that in the plural number, a number of multitude, whereby we are to understand that there was no small company of 'em.

The Christian Religion's Alliance with Folly

But not to run too far in that which is infinite. To speak briefly, all Christian Religion seems to have a kind of allyance with folly, and in no respect to have any accord with wisedom. Of which if ye expect proofs, consider first that boyes, old men, women and fools are more delighted with religious and sacred things than others, and to that purpose are ever next the Altars ; and this they do by meer impulse of Nature. And in the next place, you see that those first founders of it were plain, simple persons, and most bitter enemies of Learning. Lastly there are no sort of fools seem more out of the way than are these whom the zeal of Christian Religion has once swallow'd up ; so that they waste their estates, neglect injuries, suffer themselves to be cheated, put no difference between friends and enemies, abhor pleasure, are cram'd with poverty, watchings, tears, labours, reproaches, loathe life, and wish death above all things ; in short, they seem senseless to common underſtanding, as if their minds liv'd elsewhere and not in their own bodies ; which, what else is it than to be mad ? For which reason you muſt not think it so ſtrange if the Apoſtles seem'd to be drunk with new wine, and if Paul appear'd to Feſtus to be mad.

But now, having once gotten on the Lion's skin, go to, and I'll shew ye that this happinesse of Chriſtians, which they pursue with so much toil, is nothing else but a kind of madnesse and folly ; far be it that my words should give any offence, rather consider my matter. And firſt, the Chriſtians and Platonicks do as good as agree in this, that the Soul is plung'd and fetter'd in the prison of the body, by the grossnesse of which it is so ty'd up and hinder'd, that it cannot take a view of or enjoy things as they truly are ; and for that cause their maſter defines Philosophy to be a contemplation of death, because it takes off the mind from visible and corporeal objeᣍs, than which death does no more. And therefore, as long as the Soul useth the Organs of the Body in that right manner it ought, so long it is said to be in good ſtate and condi- tion ; but when, having broke its fetters, it endeavours to get loose, and assayes, as it were, a flight out of that prison that holds it in, they call it madness ; and if this

245

happen through any diftemper, or indisposition of the organs, then, by the common consent of every man, 'tis down-right madnesse.

And yet we see such kind of men foretell things to come, underftand Tongues and Letters they never learnt before, and seem, as it were, big with a kind of Divinity. Nor is it to be doubted but that it proceeds from hence, that the mind, being somewhat at liberty from the infection of the body, begins to put forth it self in its native vigour. And I conceive 'tis from the same cause that the like often happens to sick men a little before their death, that they discourse in ftrain above mortality, as if they were inspir'd. Agen, if this happens upon the score of Religion, though perhaps it may not be the same kind of madness, yet 'tis so near it that a great many men would judge it no better, especially when a few inconsiderable people shall differ from the reft of the world in the whole course of their life. And therefore it fares with them, as, according to the Fiction of Plato, happens to those that being coopt up in a cave ftand gaping with admiration at the shadows of things ; and that fugitive who, having broke from 'em and returning to 'em agen, told 'em he had seen things truly as they were, and that they were the moft miftaken in believing there was nothing but

pitiful shadows. For as this wise man pitty'd and bewail'd
their palpable madness that were posseſt with so grosse
an error, so they in return laught at him as a doating
fool, and caſt him out of their company.

In like manner the common sort of men chiefly admire
those things that are moſt corporeal, and almoſt believe
there is nothing beyond 'em. Whereas on the contrary,
these devout persons, by how much the nearer any thing
concerns the body, by so much the more they negleċt it,
and are wholly hurry'd away with the contemplation of
things invisible. For the one give the firſt place to riches,
the next to their corporal pleasures, leaving the laſt place
to their soul ; which yet moſt of 'em do scarce believe,
because they can't see it with their eyes. On the contrary,
the others firſt rely wholly on God, the moſt unchangeable
of all things ; and next him, yet on this that comes neareſt
him, they beſtow the second on their soul ; and laſtly,
for their body, they negleċt that care, and contemn and
fly monies as superfluity that may be well spar'd ; or if
they are forc't to meddle with any of these things, they
do it carelesly and much againſt their wills, having as if
they had it not, and possessing as if they possessed it not.

There are also in each several things several degrees
wherein they disagree among themselves. And firſt as to

the senses, though all of 'em have more or lesse affinity
with the body, yet of these some are more gross and
blockish, as tasting, hearing, seeing, smelling, touching ;
some more remov'd from the body, as memory, intellect,
and the will. And therefore to which of these the mind
applies its self, in that lyes its force. But holy men, because the whole bent of their minds is taken up with those
things that are most repugnant to these grosser senses,
they seem brutish and stupid in the common use of them.
Whereas on the contrary, the ordinary sort of people are
best at these, and can do least at t' other ; from whence
it is, as we have heard, that some of these holy men have
by mistake drunk oil for wine.

Agen, in the affections of the mind, some have a greater
commerce with the body than others, as lust, desire of
meat and sleep, anger, pride, envy ; with which holy
men are at irreconcilable enmity, and contrary, the common people think there's no living without 'em. And
lastly there are certain middle kind of affections, and as
it were natural to every man, as the love of one's Country,
Children, Parents, Friends, and to which the common
people attribute no small matter ; whereas t' other strive
to pluck 'em out of their mind : unlesse insomuch as

248

they arrive to that highest part of the soul, that they love
their Parents not as Parents—for what did they get but
the body ? though yet we owe it to God, not them—but
as good men or women, and in whom shines the Image
of that highest wisdom, which alone they call the chiefest
good, and out of which, they say, there is nothing to
be belov'd or desir'd.

And by the same rule do they measure all things else,
so that they make lesse account of whatever is visible,
unlesse it be altogether contemptible, than of those things
which they cannot see. But they say that in Sacraments
and other religious Duties there is both body and Spirit.
As in fasting they count it not enough for a man to ab-
stain from eating, which the common people take for an
absolute Fast, unlesse there be also a lessening of his
deprav'd affections : as that he be lesse angry, less proud,
than he was wont, that the Spirit, being less clog'd with
its bodily weight, may be the more intent upon heavenly
things.

In like manner, in the Eucharist, though, say they, it
is not to be esteem'd the less that 'tis administer'd with
Ceremonies, yet of its self 'tis of little effect if not hurtful,
unlesse that which is spiritual be added to it, to wit, that

which is represented under those visible signes. Now the
death of Christ is represented by it, which all men, van-
quishing, abolishing and, as it were, burying their carnal
affections, ought to express in their lives and conversa-
tions, that they may grow up to a newness of life, and
be one with him, and the same one amongst another. This
a holy man does, and in this is his only meditation.
Whereas on the contrary, the common people think there's
no more in that Sacrifice than to be present at the Altar,
and crow'd next it, to have a noise of words and look
upon the Ceremonies.

Nor in this alone, which we onely propos'd by way of
example, but in all his life, and without hypocrisie, does
a holy man fly those things that have any alliance with
the body, and is wholly ravisht with things Eternal, Invisible, and Spiritual. For which cause there's so great
contrariety of opinion between 'em, and that too in every
thing, that each party thinks the other out of their wits ;
though that character, in my judgment, better agrees with
those holy men than the common people : which yet will
be more clear if, as I promis'd, I briefly shew ye that that
great reward they so much fancy is nothing else but a
kind of madness.

The Rewards of Life Hereafter

And therefore suppose that Plato dreamt of somewhat like it when he call'd the madness of Lovers the most happy condition of all others. For he that's violently in Love lives not in his own body, but in the thing he loves ; and by how much the farther he runs from himself into another, by so much the greater is his pleasure. And then, when the mind strives to rove from its body, and does not rightly use its own organs, without doubt you may say 'tis downright madnesse and not be mistaken, or otherwise what's the meaning of those common sayings, "He does not dwell at home", "Come to your self", "He's his own man again"? Besides, the more perfect and true his love is, the more pleasant is his madness.

And therefore, what is that life hereafter, after which these holy minds so pantingly breathe, like to be ? To wit, the Spirit shall swallow up the Body, as conqueror and more durable ; and this it shall do with the greater ease because heretofore, in its life-time, it had cleans'd and thinn'd it into such another nothing as its self. And then the Spirit agen shall be wonderfully swallow'd up by that highest mind, as being more powerful than infinite parts ; so that the whole man is to be out of himself, nor to be otherwise happy in any respect, but that being ſtript of himself, he shall participate of somewhat ineffable from that chiefeſt good that draws all things into its self.

And this happiness though 'tis only then perfected when souls being joyn'd to their former bodies shall be made immortal, yet forasmuch as the life of holy men is nothing but a continu'd meditation and, as it were, shadow of that life, it so happens that at length they have some taſte or relish of it ; which, though it be but as the smalleſt drop in comparison of that fountain of eternal happiness, yet it far surpasses all worldly delight, though all the pleasures of all mankind were all joyn'd together. So much better are things spiritual than things corporal, and things invisible than things visible ; which doubtless is that which the Prophet promiseth : " The eye hath not seen, nor the ear heard, nor has it entred into the heart of man to consider what God has provided for them that love Him ". And this is that Mary's better part, which is not taken away by change of life, but perfected.

And therefore they that are sensible of it, and few there are to whom this happens, suffer a kind of somewhat little differing from madness ; for they utter many things that do not hang together, and that too not after the manner of men, but make a kind of sound which they neither

heed themselves, nor is it underſtood by others, and change
the whole figure of their countenance, one while jocund,
another while dejeƈted, now weeping, then laughing, and
agen sighing. And when they come to themselves, tell
ye they know not where they have been, whether in the
body or out of the body, or sleeping ; nor do they remember what they have heard, seen, spoken or done, and only
know this, as it were in a miſt or dream, that they were
the moſt happy while they were so out of their wits. And
therefore they are sorry they are come to themselves agen,
and desire nothing more than this kind of madnesse, to
be perpetually mad. And this is a small taſte of that future
happiness.

But I forget my self and run beyond my bounds. Though
yet, if I shall seem to have spoken any thing more boldly
or impertinently than I ought, be pleas'd to consider that
not only Folly but a Woman said it ; remembering in the
mean time that Greek Proverb, " Sometimes a fool may
speak a word in season ", unlesse perhaps you'll say this
concerns not Women. I see you expeƈt an Epilogue, but
give me leave to tell ye you are much miſtaken if you
think I remember any thing of what I have said, having
foolishly bolted out such a hodg podg of words. 'Tis an

old Proverb, " I hate one that remembers what's done over the Cup ". This is a new one of my own making : I hate a man that remembers what he hears. Wherefore farewell, clap your hands, live, and drink luſtick, my moſt excellent Disciples of Folly.

The Arsenal of Tolerance